THE INTEMPERATE PROFESSOR

RUSSELL KIRK

The Intemperate Professor

AND OTHER CULTURAL SPLENETICS

LOUISIANA STATE UNIVERSITY PRESS · BATON ROUGE

Library of Congress Catalog Card Number: 65–25673

Manufactured in the United States of America by
Kingsport Press, Inc., Kingsport, Tenn.

Designed by *Robert L. Nance*

PREFACE

Splenetic criticism is cross, crusty, and testy, of course; but also the adjective signifies remedies for an inflammation of the spleen. These studies in the afflictions of modern culture are meant as diagnoses of certain present intellectual and social discontents. Without proper diagnosis, no remedy is likely. I venture to suggest here and there, in the course of my chapters, means for the restoration of purpose and high imagination to the twentieth-century mind and heart.

The late C. E. M. Joad defined decadence as "the loss of an object." In that sense, modern civilization exhibits many signs of decadence; I examine some of these, particularly in America.

Where are we bound? Too few have been making that inquiry in this century; and the man whose curiosity on that point withers, whether from smugness or hopelessness, is decadent; for he has lost sight of the objects of life.

Exploratory rather than exhaustive, this little book pokes into certain important aspects of our civilization. The failure of our great wealth to produce greatness of mind and art; the decay of religious sentiments into mere sociability; the conversion of universities into amusement-parks, and of schoolmen into ideologues; the false premises and disastrous techniques of much schooling; the decay of apprehension of political theory; and the decline of public interest in town and country—these are some of my subjects. I describe the marks of a confused culture.

Complacency in such a time as ours is perilous. A superficial prosperity so veils our cultural sickness that old radicals like Mr. Max Lerner write smug books contending that American civilization is the summit of all human striving—and they don't intend to let anyone upset their applecart. But the Midgard serpent is gnawing at the roots of our tree of life, and unless we set our minds and consciences to the hard task of restoration and improvement, Ragnarok will not be long deferred.

Physically, modern civilization retains amazing powers of recuperation. Morally and intellectually, we are not yet bankrupt, though we have been living heedlessly upon the bank and capital of earlier and more seminal ages. A great question which we must answer in these next few years or decades is whether we still think life worth living—and if we think so, whether we still possess the talent for cultural regeneration. With a disposition to preserve, can we unite an ability to reform? Though these chapters of mine do not constitute a program for action, they may help to suggest approaches to the heart of the matter.

The word "culture" I employ as my friend T. S. Eliot used it in his *Notes Toward the Definition of Culture.* Culture is not a matter of museums and "artistic values," but rather that whole complex of imagination, sentiment, artistic achievement, and elevation of character which distinguishes the civilized man from the brute. Virility and culture are intertwined and complementary, not opposed. As modern culture decays, so modern manliness sinks; for both arise from life with dignity and purpose.

Sham leadership, sham religiosity, sham education, and sham

social progress have beset us for a good while. But in the dark wood of modern notions and infatuations, light begins to glimmer here and there. Whether we follow the corpse-candle into a cultural morass, or hit a path that leads to the realms of light, may depend on the intellectual and moral acuteness of the rising generation. Some of those who must make the grand decisions of the next ten or twenty or thirty years, I hope, may find in this book a hint or two, however badly expressed, concerning the first principles of cultural health.

Mr. Kenneth Paul Shorey helped in the preparation of the manuscript and read the proofs.

ACKNOWLEDGMENTS

Portions of this book have appeared previously in *America, Commonweal, Delta Epsilon Sigma Bulletin, Fortune, Georgia Review, Law and Contemporary Problems, Modern Age, National Review, Newman, New York Herald-Tribune Book Week, New York Times Magazine, Proceedings of the Myrin Institute, Teachers College Record, Quadrant, Southwest Review,* and *WFMT Perspective.*

Mr. Kenneth Paul Shorey helped in the preparation of the manuscript and read the proofs.

CONTENTS

COLLEGES AND CULTURE

The Intemperate
Professor

At a well-reputed private university, a faculty committee was selecting the people to be invited as guest lecturers during the next year. One member of the faculty suggested a famous professor of philosophy, Dr. Y——. This scholar, a forthright Marxian socialist, has long been associated with "liberal" and "progressive" causes. But Dr. Y—— also happens to be a courageous anticommunist, opposing the presence of communist teachers in the colleges—not merely because he disagrees with them, but because they are conspiratorial agents, discrediting the Academy and deliberately violating professional ethics.

Yet the dean of the faculty angrily vetoed the name of Dr. Y——. "What?" demanded the dean. "Y——? That Fascist reactionary? Why, he's against academic freedom." Not himself a Communist, the dean was all in favor of academic freedom: liberty, that is, for anyone not deviating from the dean's private convictions. There are no real enemies to the Left, the dean holds, and anyone who thinks otherwise ought to be considered an anathema.

College trustees, and even journalists, are often startled at the pugnacity of some professors when certain political or economic questions are raised. Frequently the social opinions of numerous American college and university teachers seem to be held with a defiant rigidity. Though these scholars may praise complete freedom of opinion in the abstract, still if someone advances an argument running counter to their political prejudices, they reach for bell, book, and candle. Having known some hundreds of professors on fifty or sixty campuses, I venture first to describe this professional intemperance and then to suggest its causes.

Writing to me about a certain "liberal" conformity in textbooks for courses in American history, Professor Stephen Graubard, a historian of science observes, "Someone ought to analyze the reasons why an entire class of scholars, teachers, and workers in the field of American history should think so much alike. The situation resembles unpleasantly the pre-revolutionary conditions at the Russian universities of Tsarist days, where faculty and students formed a hostile falange against the regime. That our American government should seem in the same position as the Tsar, is very depressing." My correspondent, born in eastern Europe, once was a Communist, and knows American campuses thoroughly. Though there is some measure of exaggeration in his comparison, it remains certain that many professors are profoundly discontented with modern American life, and endeavor to arouse a similar dissatisfaction among their students.

"He that lives in a college, after his mind is sufficiently stocked with learning," Edmund Burke wrote while he was still a young man, "is like a man who, having built and rigged a ship, should lock her up in a dry dock." Now I submit that the principal threat to academic freedom in the United States comes from dry-docked minds: the minds of "ideologues" within the walls of the Academy.

Some men who spend their lives within the Academy grow mellow; but others turn sour.

One form that such sourness takes is an incessant assertion of one's rights and a perpetual neglect of one's duties. So it comes to pass that certain of the professors, in nearly every college, who cry out most fiercely against alleged external threats to academic freedom, are in reality themselves more hostile to the liberties of the mind than is any Philistine without.

I am in the habit of calling such soured professors "the sp'iled praist" and "the stickit minister." Among the Irish, the "sp'iled praist" is a person who, having once entertained ambitions to be enrolled among the clergy, is disappointed—and so turns against all things established. Among the Scots, the "stickit minister" is a person who has lumbered halfway along the road to ordination, but has got bogged down for life, and so labors discontentedly as a dominie. Sp'iled praists and stickit ministers seldom are cheerful company. Their minds have been dry-docked; and that in rather a mean and ruinous dry dock. They put one in mind of Wordsworth's lines:

> The good die first;
> And they whose hearts are dry as summer dust
> Burn to the socket.

In university and college, especially here in America, the sp'iled praist and the stickit minister, if they turn professors, tend to become secular indoctrinators. Theirs is the glory of Cyrus P. Whittle, the Yankee schoolmaster in Santayana's novel, *The Last Puritan:* to demolish famous reputations and to expose as shams the most cherished traditions of our culture. Too many professors feel that they have been invested with the prophetic afflatus; and, having discarded theology and morals like so much antiquated rubbish, they are thrown back upon the dreary resources of twentieth-century nihilism. To feel one's self a prophet, but at the same time to insist "I am, and none else beside me," is to indulge a dangerous mood. A prophet without a gospel is worse off than a rebel without a cause. For lack of anything better, such a professor often turns to some "political religion," some ideology, as a substitute for the traditions of civility and right reason.

Most faculty members, according to Dr. George N. Shuster, president emeritus of Hunter College, have been sincerely dedicated to their profession. But their taste for a kind of secular religion also has tended sometimes toward intolerance. As Dr. Shuster writes, "Many have been or are sons of rabbis or ministers of the Gospel who have preferred secular learning to the lore of Scripture. These have given to the universities and colleges they have served a very special impulse to achieve innovation and even reform. Perhaps they are primarily responsible for a quality which no one can dissociate from the American campus and which is virtually unknown in Europe—a characteristic to be defined on the one hand as an almost bellicose addiction to freedom and on the other as a commitment to a 'liberal position,' not quite a dogma but almost one, which assays the Devil according to the degree of his 'conservatism.'"

Nowadays, the liberal or radical quasi-dogma of the bellicose professor usually is some variety of socialism, though often called "liberalism"; sometimes it goes so far as communism. But this choice of allegiance is almost accidental, dictated only by the climate of opinion in our time. In another age or country, the secular preacher in the college, the professor whose mind is in the sour dry dock, might turn to fascism, or anarchism, or Lord knows what.

The disease of our time, Edmund Burke said of his own era, is an intemperance of intellect. That is quite as true in 1965. An intemperance of intellect, which Burke called "the cause of all our other diseases," provokes the present controversy over academic freedom. Zealots of various persuasions have been attempting, sometimes with the best of intentions, to convert higher learning into an instrument for "social reconstruction," or for instilling "100% Americanism," or for "remaking human nature." Usually their endeavors are intemperate; for it is intoxicating to try to transmute Wisdom into Power. So far as academic freedom is endangered today, that freedom can be preserved only if we hold fast to an old principle: that the aim of education is the improvement of the human reason and imagination, for the individual's own sake. The Academy gained its peculiar freedom because the Academy was temperate. If the Academy becomes tipsy, blown about in every wind of doctrine, filled with professors who prefer power to wisdom, people eager to adore the idols of the marketplace, then the Academy will have lost its principle of temperance, and soon will lose its freedom.

Nearly everyone in the United States favors academic freedom—in the abstract. But the tendency of democracies to seek virtual unanimity of opinion, at every level of society, which Toc-queville saw at work long ago, continues to operate in America. For many people nowadays, among them professors, "academic free-dom" means perfect liberty to agree with *their* opinions. So long as the alleged violation of academic freedom is against a latter-day "liberal," a number of these gentlemen are ready to protest vehe-mently. But if the unfortunate is a conservative, or an old-fangled liberal, or even an anticommunist Marxist—why, what do deviation-ists like that need freedom for?

A certain college teacher of German, for instance, has been hounded out of one institution after another, by anonymous accus-ers, and by some of his colleagues. He had been so misguided as to become an obscure member of the Nazi party, in Germany—the land of his birth—in the last year of the Second World War. No one accuses him of teaching Nazi doctrines in his classes, nor even of entertaining privately, nowadays, totalitarian notions. But having once erred—though in another land, and under some compulsion—he may never be forgiven.

A case may be drawn up, of course, in defense of such severity. But *severitas* ought not to be partisan. This persecution contrasts interestingly with the impassioned defense which certain ritualistic liberals have made of former—or even present—Communists among their academic colleagues. Only one variety of totalism, we are to conclude, must be punished by exclusion from the Academy.

Real academic freedom is a right or privilege enjoyed by scholars in institutions of higher learning. The theory of academic freedom is that the search after Truth involves certain risks: for Truth is not always popular in the marketplace, and there are opinions and fields of speculation that cannot prudently be discussed in the daily press, or in public meetings. Academic freedom is intended to give the scholar a measure of security against arbitrary interference with his study and teaching—though such security never can be perfect. Now every right we enjoy has some corresponding duty. The obligation which corresponds to the right of academic freedom is this: the scholar must be dedicated to the conservation and the advancement of the Truth. He must be the guardian of the wisdom of our ancestors, and the active thinker who reconciles permanence and change in his generation. If, failing to fulfill these responsi-bilities, he becomes a propagandist, a secular indoctrinator, a man in love with power, then he falls derelict in his duty, losing his sanction for the peculiar freedom of the Academy. He ought, in short, to be a man of temperate intellect.

In American colleges today, some of the people who talk most loudly about the "menace to liberal values" are themselves intolerant of other people's opinions. According to the poet and scholar Ludwig Lewisohn, it is the "conservative professor and student, the religious professor and student" who today are a forlorn and persecuted remnant. Dr. Morton Cronin, writing in the *New Republic,* ironically says that *some* conservatives are tolerated on American campuses—so long as they are quiet, not vexing faculty meetings with their opinions. These gentlemen, Mr. Cronin adds, are the Uncle Toms of Academe; they must content themselves with saying that "they're not ashamed of being black."

One liberal professor, Dr. Ralph Gilbert Ross of the University of Minnesota, has been somewhat disquieted by the intolerance of colleagues. Writing in *Commentary,* he says that a faculty committee, of which he was a member, refused to promote a professor on the ground that he once had said something in favor of Senator Joseph McCarthy. Himself no admirer of the late Joseph McCarthy, Mr. Ross adds uneasily that perhaps this discrimination might be justified by the argument that anyone who sympathized with Senator McCarthy was stupid. But the episode affected him disagreeably, as it well might.

At a municipal college, a professor with many publications to his credit was due to receive permanent tenure of his post. A faculty committee objected to his receiving tenure. (Few of the committee members having published much, one is tempted to think of the fable of the fox and the grapes. But their charge against their colleague amounted to an accusation of personal immorality. Pressed to be more specific, they replied that the candidate was "against democracy." What did they mean? Well, said the committee sourly, the professor had written some unkind things about that democratic educator John Dewey. Their premise seems to have been that academic freedom means the liberty to agree with Dewey. In this case, despite the efforts of the faculty committee, the college's president sustained and promoted the "immoral" professor. Some twentieth-century liberals are ready to defend to the death their monopoly of the classroom. At the same time, they declare that Voltaire was a great fellow.

Their discrimination against the academic dissenter is not purely political: it extends to questions of religious belief. In many colleges, the established professorial orthodoxy is quite as intolerant of religious conviction as the medieval Church was intolerant of heresy. The Roman Catholic scholar is the worst bugaboo of such professors, but in diminished degree this hostility may extend to every variety of Christianity, excepting—and then grudgingly—only the more enthusiastic advocates of the "Social Gospel." A liberal professor of this stamp frequently equates communism and catholicism as "totalitarian movements," arguing that the Catholic scholar ought not to be admitted to the Academy because he is "committed to dogmas," and is "not his own master," and is "not free to pursue the truth wherever it may lead." (All truth, you know, leads to secularized "liberalism.") A priest in Detroit, for instance, though attached to a municipal university, was rebuffed by a professor of sociology, who refused even to argue with him in print, "because Father M—— lacks the necessary scholarly disciplines." That the priest happened also to be a doctor of philosophy of a secular university was brushed aside as an irrelevant fact: every priest, the implication ran, is by nature an ignorant obscurant.

And sometimes this discrimination is sectional, or regional, in character. The seaboard states of the Northeast, in the view of some orthodox twentieth-century liberals, are the repository of learning and enlightenment; while the wicked South is the pit of blackest ignorance and reaction. If the doctrinaire liberal never has been south of Mason and Dixon's line, his righteous prejudice is so much the stronger. He doesn't need to *see* the South; to go there would turn his stomach, he knows. He has read about the South in Mr. Erskine Caldwell's novels and has seen it depicted on Broadway; and that's evidence enough. If someone interjects that the most flourishing school of American writing today is Southern—why, the impertinent heretic must be a Fascist and a racist. An English friend of mine, new to this country, suggested to Northern liberal acquaintances that he might enroll at Duke University in North Carolina. "What?" they murmured, scandalized. "Duke? That's a *Southern* university." Such contempt sometimes extends, though not so strongly, to the Middle West. Those states, an Eastern ritualistic liberal knows, are the Bible Belt, the abode of the late Joseph McCarthy, and a cultural wasteland. Even scholars of outwardly tolerable views, if they come from this desolation, may be suspect as corrupted by prairie bigotry, until they have demonstrated the contrary.

But above and beyond politics and religion and region, the all-embracing conformity exacted by the ritualistic liberals is conformity to the doctrine of "non-commitment." A scholar, these gentlemen argue, ought to be committed to no firm point of view about anything. Though he ought to pursue Truth, he must never embrace her. His mind, like that of John Locke's infant, ought to be a blank tablet, so far as first principles of morals and politics and taste are concerned. He should doubt all things, for the sake of doubting; he should break down old prejudices in students' minds. Nothing is settled, or ought to be; the function of the university is to "destroy all barriers to the questing spirit of man." At a state college in Michigan, certain professors of education, sociology, and psychology—dedicated liberals all—drew up an elaborate set of tests to be administered to all entering freshmen and all graduating seniors, for determining their "value preferences" and "environmental prejudices," and how efficaciously the college does its good work of eradicating stubborn convictions acquired from tradition and family instruction.

One of these tests included a question as to whether the student believed that "it is wrong for a brother to have sexual relations with his sister." The student who replied "yes" was classified, so far as this question went, as inclined toward irrational prejudices. Not that the liberal professors were in favor of incest on principle; they said they were in favor of nothing on principle; they simply aspired to "give the student an open mind" and "set free the inquiring rationality." When the tests were analyzed, they found, presumably to their sorrow, that graduating seniors left college with the very prejudices they had entertained as freshmen: the college had failed in its mission.

Whether the liberal professors really act upon this absolute relativism is another matter. At an Ohio university, a decade ago, some of these scholars proposed that all members of the faculty be required to vow that they would teach only by "the empirical method." This, it turned out, meant the philosophical and social principles of John Dewey. Only after heated debate was the proposal defeated. In politics, the ritualistic liberals affirm, a scholar ought to have no commitments—except, that is, to democracy and liberalism. Strong affirmation of faith in democracy and liberalism isn't commitment; it's merely the Truth. And who defines democracy and liberalism? A faculty committee of latter-day liberals. Who else could?

At one great university, a conservative scholar was proposed for an appointment. No, never, said the doctrinaire liberals: he's committed to a "point of view." They wouldn't for the world think of depriving him of his right to express that point of view—except at their university. Some brave soul suggested, at this moment, that the faculty already included several eminent men of the Left. "Nonsense!" said the majority; commitment in *that* direction—well, it's harmless anyway.

Here I have set down some fragmentary evidence of the malady of the intemperate professor. Upon many American campuses, the prevailing climate of opinion remains—if modified—still a quasi-collectivistic liberalism, among faculty politicians and those energetic persons who push themselves to the headships of lecture committees and tenure committees. Theirs is a wondrously illiberal liberalism. The most charitable view a dispassionate observer can take of these gentlemen is that they do not understand the meaning of their own favorite word "liberal." At a Wisconsin college, some young instructors objected to having any known conservative speak on the campus, because "this is a *liberal* arts college." Conceivably they really were ignorant that political liberalism is much younger than the liberal arts—unaware that the liberal education which John Henry Newman praised is quite different from the partisan social liberalism which Newman detested.

A gentleman with considerable experience of our universities observes to me that many professors really are not interested in academic freedom, however great an outcry they make about alleged threats to their right to free expression. What some professors really mean when they say "academic freedom" is academic power. They do not truly desire to conserve or extend the realm of Truth, or to teach a body of knowledge to intelligent students. What they really desire is authority to bend their colleagues and their students to their own will. They seek to compel colleagues, students, and society to submit to some ideology; and even that ideology is not so important to them as the sense of power which accompanies this opportunity to propagandize, to indoctrinate, to alter society and human nature radically. Men generally are too fond of power. Harder to repress than lechery or gluttony or avarice, this lust for power is the strongest of vices. But the scholar professes to have given up his claim to power in favor of the service of Truth. And so a professor lusting after power, under the cloak of academic freedom, converts liberty into license. He is not truly seeking freedom either for himself or for others, such a power-tipsy professor; he really wishes to impose his own will and opinions, without much scruple, upon whoever happens to fall within his influence.

I am not saying that this fault of intemperance afflicts *most* American professors. The majority of them are tolerant enough, interested in their discipline rather than in power. Nor am I saying that intemperance and power-lust are peculiar to *American* professors; as Raymond Aron suggests in his book *The Opium of the Intellectuals,* this situation has been at least as bad in the French universities; and I have met at Oxford colleges certain influential professors who are quite as politically dogmatic and impatient of contradiction as are their American counterparts. I am saying only that on many of our campuses the belligerent political radical or antireligious zealot has an influence out of proportion to the numerical strength of his clique. And I am trying to analyze the reasons for this intemperance of intellect.

A well-known economist, Professor Ludwig von Mises, tells us that American intellectuals have an "anti-capitalist mentality." Living in a competitive society, which offers large rewards to practical abilities, we Americans pay the professor less well, in money and status, than certain other societies have rewarded him. In the United States, Dr. Mises suggests, the intellectual rarely is invited to mingle with the rich, famous, and powerful; feeling neglected, he develops a deep resentment against "capitalism," attributing to free enterprise his own unprosperous condition. Though his own mentality is distinctly procapitalist, Professor Mises sees no remedy for this prejudice on the part of American professors; he implies only that we ought to keep these envious folk from exercising power. "To understand the intellectual's abhorrence of capitalism," Mises writes, "one must realize that in his mind this system is incarnated in a definite number of compeers whose success he resents and whom he makes responsible for the frustration of his own farflung ambitions. His passionate dislike of capitalism is a mere blind for his hatred of some successful 'colleagues.'"

Envy being part of original sin, it is perhaps inevitable that a twentieth-century professor of envious disposition should attribute his discontent to the workings of the profit motive, quite as it was tempting for an envious scholar of the Dark Ages to attribute his comparative failure to the workings of Satan. Every age has its devils and its whipping boys. Yet, though unconscious or half-conscious envy certainly is a factor in the mentality of the Academy's sp'iled praists and stickit ministers, I think there are other causes for their attitude; and there may be remedies.

Among the tangle of causes for sour discontent in the Academy, four seem especially powerful. These may be described as Frozen Liberalism, the Chaotic Campus, the Depression Mentality, and the Utopian Delusion.

By Frozen Liberalism, I mean that many college teachers formed their opinions—or got them ready-made—thirty or forty years ago, and have refused to alter them since. Thinking always is painful, and why should a professor be expected to suffer? A European intellectual who often lectures in America, Dr. Erik von Kuehnelt-Leddihn, speaks ironically of a "Holy Liberal Inquisition" which dominates a great many American campuses: every scholar is expected by the Inquisitors of One-Hundred-Per-Cent Liberalism to subscribe to their secular catechism, or else be anathema. Recently, for instance, Dr. Glenn Campbell was appointed to the headship of the Hoover Institution at Stanford University. No sooner had he arrived than the local liberal inquisitors asked if he had any sympathy with the political and economic views of Mr. Herbert Hoover, founder of the institution. When they discovered him so heretical as to express substantial agreement with Mr. Hoover, they persuaded the Stanford faculty senate to pass a resolution—by a narrow majority—denouncing the appointment of Dr. Campbell.

These Inquisitors—many less courteous than the monks who interrogated Galileo—often are gentlemen who read the *Nation* and the *New Republic* from cover to cover in the twenties and thirties—and have read little since. For them, liberalism is a closed and immutable system, easily expressed in journalists' phrases. Franco-Spain is Hell, and the Chinese communists still are simple agrarian reformers. In such attitudes, they have much in common with the Depression Mentality I describe below; but the distinguishing characteristic of these frozen liberals is their inverted conservatism. They seem resolved that no doctrine of an origin more recent than their own graduate school years should be discussed on an

American campus. The revival of conservative political and economic ideas is especially shocking to them, but they have their own conservatism.

This conservatism of mental indolence and jealous self-interest is no new phenomenon; in one form or another, it has existed among institutionalized scholars ever since the schools of Plato and Aristotle arose. Nowadays, because the dominant orthodoxy of a generation ago was Ritualistic Liberalism, the inverted conservatism of these professors is Frozen Liberalism. Though they profess to be haters of all things established, these scholars actually detest any change in their own disciplines or in the social opinions they acquired in youth. Mr. Arthur Koestler, in his recent book, *The Sleepwalkers,* describes the trial of Galileo and observes, in passing, that "professionals with a vested interest in tradition and in the monopoly of learning" always tend to block the development of new concepts. So the Aristotelian scholars in the seventeenth-century universities dealt intolerantly with Galileo. "Innovation is a twofold threat to academic mediocrities: it endangers their oracular authority, and it evokes the deeper fear that their whole laboriously constructed intellectual edifice might collapse. The academic backwoodsmen have been the curse of genius from Aristarchus to Darwin and Freud. . . ." The intemperate Frozen Liberals of the American campus in 1965 are just such academic backwoodsmen.

By the Chaotic Campus, I mean the mass scale, the confusion, and the lowering of standards which afflict most American campuses nowadays. Swollen by the "rising tide" of enrollments since the Second World War, American universities and colleges are bursting with prosperity—of a sort. Whatever the benefit of conferring degrees upon a proportion of the population three times as large as used to attend college, this process of sudden expansion has tended to dehumanize the college. All activity—except at such liberal arts colleges as mean to hold the line against mass growth—is more and more standardized, but not more and more orderly. The businesslike administrative officers of the college increase in importance; the scholarly professor slides toward the status of a hired hand. Many students enroll only for a snob degree, urged on by parents, or for four years of dating and sports cars. Some are incapable of real college study; others are unwilling to make the effort genuine study exacts. Although I cannot enter here into the complex ills of the college boom, I suggest that this partial collapse of order and discipline in our colleges, this break with the quiet life which used to be general on American campuses, distresses and alienates some able teachers.

For the professor by nature is attached to order. He professes a regular discipline. He believes in intellectual standards. When the time is out of joint, especially on his campus, he is badly disquieted. He never expected to grow rich by teaching; but he did expect a fairly leisurely, retired, respected profession. He did not contract to be ordered about by a college administrative bureaucracy, or to put up with insolent, indolent, and sometimes fraudulent students. All about him he sees confusion nowadays; and sometimes he attributes this confusion, this loss of his old status, to the political system and the economy which govern our modern nation. He protests against this chaotic change by appealing to a "liberal" ideology, perhaps— even though triumph of the sort of liberalism he adores might aggravate, really, the campus confusion.

This Chaotic Campus is an affliction of the past fifteen years, mainly, though its roots go back to the beginning of this century. Some intelligent people are already doing what they can to remedy its worst aspects. In his essay on "Academic Leisure," more than fifty years ago, Irving Babbitt of Harvard gloomily described the "humanitarian hustling" in American colleges: the passion for attempting everything, hurriedly and superficially; the tendency for the college to try to be all things to all men—and to deprive the scholar of his rightful and necessary intellectual leisure. "Of action we shall have enough in any case," Babbitt concluded, "but it is only by a more humane reflection that we can escape the penalties sure to be exacted from any country that tries to dispense in its national life with the principle of leisure."

Here I suggest only that the sourness and resentment of some American professors nowadays is in consequence of this "humanitarian hustling" on the campus—our swollen enrollments, our disregard of real standards, our indifference to the claims of the scholar. And I put the question that an extending of higher schooling to many more young people may become a national injury, rather than a general improvement, if those young people are taught superficially by professors who have been alienated from our society by the very process of rapid expansion on the campus.

One instructor in English literature whom I know has his students read the books of Mickey Spillane, as principal examples of twentieth-century writing. It isn't that the professor admires *Kiss Me, Deadly* or its author: no, he says that "Spillane is a Fascist." Yet Mickey Spillane, my acquaintance declares, is a typical specimen of the modern America—decadently tough, loveless, aimless, seeking escape in violence. Spillane represents disorder; therefore the professor—very much a dry-docked mind—orders his students to read Spillane, as "contemporary literature," presumably that they may learn how evil our society has become and how it ought to be supplanted by a "new order." When I hear well-meaning people argue that simple quantitative growth of enrollments is bound to improve American culture and politics, I think of this professor and his influence. No small amount of professors' intemperance is provoked by the disorderly campus of 1965.

By the Depression Mentality, I mean that the majority of today's college teachers—the professors in their forties—attended high school and college during the era of the Great Depression; and some of them cling fondly to the slogans and attitudes of those turbulent years. The New Deal, the Popular Front, the leagues against war and fascism, the bewildering kaleidoscope of proposals for radical social change which were brought forward as early as 1929 and endured into the forties—with these, the present generation of professors grew up intellectually. And not a few of them grew up, also, with a haunting sense of economic and psychological insecurity, conscious of the "underprivileged" and the "malefactors of great wealth" and all that—sometimes identifying themselves with the idealized Common Man.

As in that penetrating but short-lived Broadway play, *The Egghead,* many a professor of this day is fixed emotionally to the political and intellectual commitments of his undergraduate days. "Prevailing opinions," Disraeli wrote more than a century ago, "generally are the opinions of the generation that is passing." The problems of 1965 are not precisely the problems of 1932; but some college teachers grow vexed when their students decline to share their enthusiasms for the causes of yesteryear. In practical politics, a goodly number of professors think we still are fighting the battles of the Hoover and Roosevelt administrations; though they fancy themselves a daring *avant-garde,* in actuality they are tearfully nostalgic. Looking for a second Franklin Roosevelt to lead them to Zion, some long for positions of authority in Washington, another rally of brain trusters. For a time, many saw such a leader in Adlai Stevenson;

later, they turned to Senator Hubert Humphrey, who had been a professor himself. I know of private and state colleges in which the whole faculty of certain departments swore by Humphrey, urging their students to campaign for him. They not only wanted Mr. Humphrey for president, but were thoroughly convinced that the Common Man would nominate and elect him. Their chagrin after the West Virginia primary in 1960 was not pretty to look upon.

Professor Moses Hadas, an elderly classicist, laments the fact that his students have turned conservative. Years ago, he says, he used to tell his classes about Agis and Cleomenes, the radical reforming kings of Sparta who came to a miserable end for the sake of a dream; but his students of today—unlike students of a generation gone, who desired to emulate the Spartans—think Agis and Cleomenes were fools. Certainly radicalism does not thrive among college students as it did in the confused and ideologue-plagued thirties; and this student hostility to radical innovation disturbs and sometimes infuriates nostalgic professors. "Why, these youngsters think we're old fogies," the chairman of a department of English said to me. "They just don't go for the causes that used to excite us." If you have thought you were leading a triumphal march toward a Brave New World, with the students at your back, and then glance around to find that, instead, you have turned your back on the students; if you find yourself middle-aged and rather lonely, and unable to understand the rising generation that was supposed to require your leadership—why, you may have some excuse for a jaundiced disposition.

This source of alienation among professors will work its own cure, for the graduate students of the sixties—the professors of the seventies and eighties—will have their roots in the Eisenhower era; and whatever their deficiencies, they are unlikely to hold many illusions about Soviet Russia, or to cherish the memory of Harry Hopkins and Henry Wallace. But the ill feeling of certain professors against an era which failed to become the Century of the Common Man will persist until they add emeritus to their titles. Marx and Freud, names dear to the young intellectuals of the twenties, will yield pride of place to other seminal minds. That is the way of the world, but the dry-docked professor resents the nature of things.

By the Utopian Delusion, I mean the notion that somehow human existence ought to be perfectly happy, and since it is not nowadays, the System or perhaps "wicked reactionaries" are to blame. This doctrine of the perfectibility of man and society is derived from the Enlightenment of the eighteenth century; it is at loggerheads with the Christian belief that human nature necessarily is flawed and that perfect happiness cannot be attained in this world, man being incurably restless and insatiable here below. To enjoy Heaven here and now, to create the Terrestrial Paradise—this is the ambition of the Utopian intellectual.

Modern society is riddled with imperfections; so all societies have ever been. But modern society also has certain considerable merits, and these the Utopian professor among us usually has ignored. In economics, for instance, he has behaved as if wealth were somehow the gift of nature, and if we could arrange for the government to distribute it equally, human perfection would be at hand. Though the terrible events of the twentieth century have disconcerted many scholars who formerly believed in the march of Progress with a capital P, something of their hope for the earthly paradise lingers on—and something, also, of their anger with the vested interests who, they think, are bent upon thwarting the aspirations of the Common Man.

Since the Russian Revolution, this Utopian impulse usually has taken the form of sympathy with communism. Not more than 5 percent of American college teachers ever were Communists, though the number of fellow travelers was considerably greater; and since the Second World War, the hard core of Communists has shrivelled. Yet there endures on the campus a kind of sneaking sympathy with revolutionaries who profess doctrines of total equality, so that gentlemen like Dr. Castro still have their panegyrists.

If one is to believe a certain survey of academic opinion,[1] nearly one quarter of our teachers of social science in college appear to be determined radicals. The percentage of radicalism also runs fairly high in departments of English, to judge from my own observations. I am not sure why, though it is conceivably because many professors of English literature permit a vague sentimentality to do duty for a serious understanding of politics.

Although the primary function of the professor is to pass on to the rising generation a body of knowledge, it is true that the professor has the right, and even the duty, to criticize his age. Colleges ought not to be centers for smugness. But from lively criticism to indoctri-

[1] Paul F. Lazarsfeld and Wagner Thielens, Jr., *The Academic Mind* (Glencoe, Illinois, 1958).

nation for revolutionary change may be a dangerous leap. Our civil social order, with its high degree of justice and freedom, with its guarantees of human dignity, has been slowly and painfully created by thousands of years of historical experience, trial and error. The imprudent Utopian professor can do great mischief to enthusiastic and impressionable young people by inculcating among them a sneering and sullen mood, by setting for them social goals impossible to attain. Burke called the Jacobin radicalism of the French Revolution "the revolt of the enterprising talents of a nation against its property." The thoroughgoing Utopian professor would like to do just that—to make of his students sullen or rash rebels against everything established. To live with a gnawing grudge against one's own civilization is the way to a personal Hell, not to the Terrestrial Paradise.

Personally, indeed, some of the Utopian intellectuals are markedly unattractive. One professor of my acquaintance is given to long discourses in praise of universal brotherhood and the welfare state. But when some unlucky student presents him with note cards incorrectly arranged, the humanitarian scholar flings the lot of them on the classroom floor, contemptuously, and watches the student pick them up. This professor says he detests "the authoritarian personality" and desires complete democracy, economic as well as political. Yet he might not have done badly as a commissar or a gauleiter; for some of those gentleman, too, commenced as Utopian intellectuals.

During the next few decades, I suspect, there will be less talk in the Academy about marching to the earthly Zion and more attention to the norms of morals and politics and taste, from which we derive order in personality and justice in society. I think we are going to see more intelligently conservative professors. The Academy is beginning to regain its balance, to revive the pagan virtue of temperance.

The degree of academic freedom which any educational system can sustain always depends upon the general soundness and thoroughness of that educational system. If the professor is a half-educated man, intoxicated by a little learning and convinced that, out of his omniscience, he has the duty to impose his convictions upon his students; if the student is ill-grounded and unable even to read critically—why, then the free exchange of opinions, founded upon the assumption that professors are servants of truth and that students are competent to distinguish between falsity and right reason, becomes almost impossible. The intemperate professor, the presumptuous "intellectual," becomes the secular indoctrinator; and the student becomes his dupe. In America, this problem of academic freedom will be solved only by a restoration of real learning, at every level of schooling.

The sp'iled praist and the stickit minister in the Academy are inhumane: that is, they have forgotten the purposes of the Academy. For the truth of ethical and intellectual attainment, they have substituted the illusion of Utopian social reconstruction. What example a teacher sets is quite as important as what he teaches. While a temperate and generous mind can wake the best in the rising generation, a sour and carping view of life can warp the character of college students.

Such, down to our time, is the ancient contest between philosopher and philodoxer. Gradual disillusion with ideology may be the salvation of the Academy's temperance. "Intelligence will tell in the long run," a Harvard colleague said once to Irving Babbitt, "even in a university." Aye, intelligence—with a dash of humility.

May Professors
Profess Principles?

O n March 7, 1959, the *Saturday Evening Post* published an article with the title, "Are We Making a Playground out of College?" Jerome Ellison, an associate professor of journalism at Indiana University, wrote it. On January 9, 1960, a second article by Mr. Ellison appeared in the *Post*—"American Disgrace: College Cheating." Shortly before the second article came out, Professor Ellison was given notice by the university, and will teach no more at Bloomington.

While in itself an interesting case, this dismissal of a well-known

21

writer and teacher has a larger significance. It is one engagement in a struggle fought for the past several years on hundreds of college campuses—particularly, as Mr. Ellison suggests, at the "Big Ten" universities and other middle western institutions. On one side are certain college administrators interested primarily in larger enrollments; on the other, college professors interested primarily in the works of the mind.

During the next decade, the controversy about academic freedom may shift from the debate concerning Communist and fellow-traveling teachers to a fierce argument over whether professors have the right to uphold intellectual standards.

That Mr. Ellison was dismissed because he had presumed to criticize the "Second Curriculum" at American universities seems to be established beyond reasonable doubt. His observations had included some passing comments on life at Indiana University—though only as one among many campuses.

Five years earlier, the university had engaged Mr. Ellison as a teacher of journalism. His qualifications were remarkably good: he had been managing editor of *Collier's* and editor of *Liberty*. His performance as a teacher at Indiana seems to have been superior: his student editorial team won the national college yearbook championship; many of his students placed their writings in national magazines; he was commended for proficiency in teaching journalism by a national accreditation committee; and he published more articles of his own than did his eight departmental colleagues combined. With his wife, he founded a successful national magazine, *Best Articles and Stories*, which reprinted selections from scholarly and critical quarterlies. He was promoted from assistant to associate professor. In two more years, he would have acquired tenure at the university. But then he trod upon the perilous ground of educational criticism.

To suggest that anything might conceivably be unsatisfactory at one of our great state universities now requires some boldness in a professor at such an institution. Not many take the risk—especially if they have two years to go before they obtain tenure. Mr. Ellison wrote in his first *Post* article:

Entering the academic life from the "outside world," one is disappointed by the banality of conversation at social gatherings, and by attitudes of old-fashioned trade-unionism centering on "tenure," a word which means that after they've kept you on for seven years it's almost impossible for them to fire you. This concern for tenure bends many teachers toward cautious utterance, often blunting the kind of searching, outspoken discourse that might explode into exciting teaching and learning.

Once his article on college playgrounds was published, the administrators of the university made it clear to Professor Ellison that his brand of outspoken discourse was not desired at Bloomington. The university's public relations bureau burst into activity, sending out news releases hostile to Mr. Ellison and angry letters against him, including a demand to the *Post* that the editors apologize for publishing such stuff—on pain, it was hinted, of retaliation against the magazine. The president of Indiana University, Dr. Herman Wells, personally directed the preparation of a dossier questioning Mr. Ellison's personal integrity and professional competence.

Ellison chose, according to the dean of the graduate school, "to pander to an insatiable appetite for the comic strip and Hollywood version of college life." The acting dean of students cried out that Ellison's work was "a lot of bosh," and that Ellison was "searching for sensationalism." The university's public-relations chief diligently publicized these temperate comments. An Indianapolis newspaper columnist wrote, shortly after Mr. Ellison's first article was published, that he had "official word" Ellison would be dropped from the Indiana faculty in punishment. Soon other university administrators joined in the chorus against Mr. Ellison, though a number of their complaints seem curiously irrelevant to what he had written in the *Post*.

Some students hanged Professor Ellison in effigy before the journalism building. "Apparently I have arrived," Mr. Ellison observed. "I stand on my thirty years' work and my record for integrity. I said what I had to say in that article."

By the middle of December, the Department of Journalism decided that Professor Ellison's contract would not be renewed, because the tenure members of the department had concluded that "the teaching, counseling, and sharing of duties [by Mr. Ellison] did not meet the requirements we wanted in a person retained on a permanent basis." They added that of course Mr. Ellison's *Post* article had nothing to do with their action.

President Wells was even more emphatic on this point. "I'm absolutely confident," he said in a statement for the student newspaper, "the article did not have anything to do with his not being re-appointed. This office simply takes the recommendations of the department in all such matters." It was Dr. Wells who had ordered the preparation of documents against Mr. Ellison. In the Indiana faculty handbook is this passage concerning academic freedom: "No restraint shall be placed upon the teacher's freedom in investigation. . . . In speaking and writing outside of the institution upon subjects beyond the scope of his own field of study [the teacher] is entitled to precisely the same freedom, but is subject to the same responsibility as attaches to all other citizens." But the administrators at Bloomington gave Professor Ellison the freedom to do his writing somewhere else—if he could find a post. The widely-circulated press releases against him might injure his opportunities elsewhere; and there have been attempts, sometimes successful, to blacklist stubborn professors who resign or are dismissed.

Mr. Ellison is one of the best-known professors of journalism in America. Until he published his *Post* article, he was given no notice that his work at Indiana seemed unsatisfactory to the administrative hierarchy. Having looked carefully into this case, I am convinced that Professor Ellison was discharged simply because he had the effrontery to criticize many American colleges and universities, including his own, in a popular magazine.

Now what outrageous charges did Mr. Ellison make against higher learning in America? If one takes the trouble to read his article on college playgrounds, one finds a temperate, sincere, well-documented account of the "Second Curriculum" at the great majority of our colleges and universities. My own observations—and I have visited more than a hundred campuses—coincide with Mr. Ellison's. And I doubt that any competent professor of arts or science can deny, to himself at least, the truth of what Mr. Ellison writes.

The Second Curriculum is the fun fair which overshadows book learning. It is the marriage-market, the athletics craze, the passion for snap courses. In Mr. Ellison's words, it

is that odd mixture of status hunger, voodoo, tradition, lust, stereotyped dissipation, love, solid achievement, and plain good fun sometimes called "college life." It drives a high proportion of our students through college chronically short of sleep, behind in their work, and uncertain of the exact score in any department of life.

With examples from many campuses—chiefly from state universities—Mr. Ellison combines information from various reliable surveys of the state of our colleges, notably the Hazen Foundation report, *Changing Values in College*. His purpose is not mere denunciation, but rather the restoration of first principles in higher education. He puts this very well, toward the end of his second *Post* article:

The first step in a school concerned about its cheating, I would think, should be to ask itself what it stands for. Does it rest its reputation on having the biggest enrollment in its state? As fielding the best football team? As offering the greatest variety of courses? As having the handsomest fraternity houses and the most luxurious student-union building? None of these things, I suggest, offers the kind of challenge required. The school must assign itself some inspired goal, some lofty set of aims which has won the passionate loyalty of a dedicated faculty. These aims, whatever may be their specific nature, should have their roots in an undeviating allegiance to the truth.

The practical, national importance of truth is, I think, too little recognized. I am speaking now, not of ideals that tend to become fuzzily poetic, but of the hardheaded business of getting along in the job of being a nation.

Mr. Ellison's prudence and good nature impress me; there is in his articles nothing of the "sensationalism" which the deans at Indiana professed to find. But I do not propose here to open the general question of the effects of the Second Curriculum. My immediate point is that many able American professors, of whom Mr. Ellison is a representative specimen, are convinced that intellectual and moral standards have suffered a marked decline in our colleges since World War Two; and that many American college and university administrators shut their eyes to this decline, being intent on bigger enrollments; and—this last being my main theme—that some of the administrators have made up their minds to close the mouths of the protesting professors.

This struggle between administrators and teachers obtains public attention only rarely. For the majority of professional objectors to the lowering of standards and the disregard of traditional disciplines do nothing but grumble with their colleagues. "This is a city of brave children and timid men," a nonacademic friend once said to me as we walked the streets of a college town. The permissively reared

professors' children swaggered past us; but the professors themselves
looked excessively meek—not with the meekness of Moses, or of the
sort that shall inherit the earth. To protest, even in a faculty meeting,
against the Second Curriculum, the prevalence of cheating, or the
proliferation of trifling courses may provoke the frowns of president
and deans; and that can mean a teacher might be passed over for
advancement, or—like Mr. Ellison—suddenly be found wanting in
pedagogical techniques and counseling skills. Once I was present,
and vocal, at a faculty meeting in which a half-dozen professors,
indeed, ventured to speak against a proposed lowering of grade
standards. As each of the objectors rose, a cynical colleague at my
elbow murmured, "He's a full professor, with tenure," or, "He's a
single man."

When a scholar does have sufficient resolution to object, within or
without a college, to the decay of higher learning, a few people hear
about it—or about what warnings to him or positive measures of
retaliation may have come from the college administration. I describe several such instances in my book *Academic Freedom* (1955).
The administrators of the state universities and colleges have at their
service an elaborate and well-paid public relations bureau; the
average professor is obscure enough, without friends among the
newspaper editors or the members of the state legislature. As Toc-
queville says of the dissenter under democratic despotism, he may
find himself deserted by his former friends, crushed by the weight of
a vague disapproval rather than by positive punishments, and so
regret that he ever spoke out.

Yet occasionally some single combat in this contest between
empire-building administrators and intellect-respecting professors
comes to public attention. Before the Ellison case, the most startling
episode of this sort in recent years occurred at the University of
Nevada, in 1953. There Dr. Frank Richardson, a professor of biology,
was summarily dismissed by the university's president, Dr. (of education) Minard Stout, because he had ventured to distribute among
the faculty copies of a pamphlet by Professor Arthur Bestor, *Aimless-
ness in Education*—and because Dr. Richardson was known to
believe in reasonably high academic standards. After prolonged
controversy and litigation, the supreme court of Nevada ordered Dr.
Richardson's reinstatement, because he had possessed tenure; a
committee appointed by the Nevada legislature reported against
President Stout; the people of Nevada elected new university

regents, who removed Stout from the presidency. Even though Dr. Richardson meanwhile had left Reno for less troubled waters, this was a real victory for academic freedom. But it occurred only because of Dr. Richardson's courage and persistence.

Generally it is less injurious for a professor to be accused of communist sympathies than for him to be found wanting in enthusiasm for indiscriminate expansion of college enrollments. If he is in danger of dismissal for his radicalism, often a crowd rushes to his defense: a considerable segment of the press, eminent liberal politicians and publicists, the American Association of University Professors (AAUP), the Civil Liberties Union. But if he has clashed with president and dean over academic standards, he may find no one interested except his nervous family. Much of the public does not understand the issue at all, and can be easily won to the administrators' side by facile slogans about how "our wonderful boys and girls deserve college educations, as many of them as we can find room for." Even the AAUP has been markedly reluctant to intervene in such controversies.

And the public assumes, usually, that the administrators know best; so, too, most of the alumni assume; so, perhaps, the college trustees or the educational committees of the state legislature. A college president is Constituted Authority—with a public relations bureau next door; a professor is only an impractical intellectual, probably full of crotchets.

What the public and the alumni and the trustees and the legislators often forget is that university administrators, like the rest of us, are afflicted by the *libido dominandi.* Swelling college enrollments mean more divisions and departments for an administrator to control; more faculty appointments at his disposal; handsome new buildings on his campus; a larger body of alumni, eventually, through whom he can exert influence; perhaps a larger salary for himself; certainly more attention in the newspapers. It is not easy for an administrator to resist these temptations; and it is so unpleasant to be thinking all the time about high standards and old disciplines, and so convenient not to know exactly what goes on in crowded classrooms. So the interest of an administrator need not always coincide with the interest of his faculty, or of the students (at least the more serious students among them), or of the university's intellectual reputation, or—in the long run—of the public. And this divergence of interest comes about the more easily if the administrator is not

himself educated in any genuinely humane or scientific discipline,
but has been trained only in administrative methods, technical skills,
or "education" (Teachers' College variety).

I am not saying that the crotchety professor always is right, or that
the harried administrator always is wrong. There are teachers whose
chief delight it is to vex presidents and deans simply by way of
passing the time, while some of my better friends are college
administrators—and are as devoted to decent standards as is the
most tradition-directed professor. The flood of students into our
colleges and universities since World War Two has created problems
that demand fresh approaches.

But I am saying that professors ought to be allowed to discuss
these real problems and to be protected in their right to criticize
reasonably the ends and means of college administrators. If scholars
and teachers have no freedom to discuss educational standards,
whatever is academic freedom meant for? It is important, I know,
that professors enjoy a high degree of freedom of expression upon
political questions. But it is still more important that they be free to
affirm their educational first principles. If political expression is
curbed, only those teachers interested in politics are directly affected; but if educational opinions are repressed, every conscientious
teacher is at once injured. Politics, after all, is a secondary concern
for the professor: he does not rule the state. Educational ends and
means, however, are the primary concern of the professor: they
constitute the essence of his vocation. If he is not free to criticize the
standards of the university, he enjoys no real liberty—nor will he be
competent to impart intellectual disciplines meant for free men.

Professor Ellison's very readable articles, founded upon personal
observation, are precisely the sort of discussion our university
administrators ought to encourage. The president or dean who flies
into a rage at such criticism must suffer from a bad conscience, I
suspect. Mr. Ellison makes a number of practical proposals for
reform. These his administrative adversaries do not deign to examine. Bigotry is nowhere more destructive than at the top of a
foundation for higher learning.

In the *Gorgias*, Socrates remarks that most men do not take
kindly to the preacher of moral reform, the pursuer of the good.
"There is no telling," Socrates says, "what may happen to such a
man." What the possessors of administrative power have done to
Professor Ellison is quite clear: they have deprived him of his post

and have tried to injure his reputation. Similar things will happen, these next few years, to other preachers of educational reform. For there are among us certain titular guardians of the Academy who conceal the decay of learning, condone cheating, and consign to the outer darkness the conscientious teacher.

*Massive Subsidies
and Academic Freedom*

*T*o kill through kindness is quite possible. Although some of the old causes of insecurity in academic freedom have diminished considerably in recent years, new influences are at work which—even granting the benignity of the intentions involved—may produce difficulties less susceptible of remedy.

As Tocqueville remarked of "democratic despotism," the impalpable pressures of a prosperous mass society can be more oppressive ultimately—and harder to resist successfully—than the arbitrary measures of the autocracies of yesteryear. The English and Scottish universities have endured through the centuries—most of the time—with a high degree of academic freedom, in considerable part because their permanent endowments were sufficient to provide for their annual expenditures. (Only since World War Two have they come to depend for half their revenues upon government grants.) It is only seemingly a paradox that in a "democratic" age educational institutions are better provided with cash than ever they were before—and yet exhibit less independence and strength of opinion than they did in less egalitarian times.

For no proverb is truer than this, "The man who pays the piper calls the tune." If educational institutions become dependent for their increase of reputation, or perhaps even for their existence, upon a few sources of benefaction, ineluctably most administrators and even professors will play their pipes accordingly. And this is not the less true merely because a government is "democratic," or a foundation "charitable." Governments and foundations are directed by men, with prejudices and interests like all of us—which may not always be identical with the opinions and advantages of the more lively spirits in the Academy.

President Nathan S. Pusey, of Harvard University, recently spoke of certain distortions suffered by his university because of its participation in federal programs of scientific research. Institutions less well prepared to defend themselves than Harvard may experience greater discomfort, when confronting the benefactions and the demands of the Department of Defense or of the Ford Foundation. At the University of Louisville, for instance, all eight doctoral programs in the graduate school are scientific, and are subsidized—nay, originated—by federal governmental activities. Need one labor the point that, potentially, a university is less free to make its own important decisions under such circumstances?

Rather than analyzing at this moment the theoretical perils to academic freedom from such concentration of power, I offer some very recent case histories. The dangers to academic freedom are not remote: already, in certain institutions, conformity to the preferences and value judgments of the administrators of foundations and governmental agencies is being enforced. I refrain from naming institutions and scholars involved, because that would increase their difficulties. This point was made recently by Dr. John A. Howard,[1] president of Rockford College:

[1] John A. Howard, in *Widening Horizons,* Newsletter, Rockford College, Ill., April, 1963, p. 3.

This is not a chimera born of a doctrinaire distrust of government. Recently I wrote to the president of a large well-known university inviting him to join a group of college presidents in making known the arguments against the ever-growing federal subsidies of education. He replied that although he was in full agreement with our position, that the subsidies are not in the long-range best interest of the colleges or the country, his own university was now so dependent upon funds from Washington that he could not exercise his rights as a citizen on this issue without jeopardizing the university he served.

Such uneasiness among university and college presidents may be discerned in their relationships with the great foundations, too. Some years ago, I addressed a national educational society—touching in my remarks, incidentally, upon the ideas of the former president of a foundation which, just a few weeks earlier, had bestowed large subsidies upon many colleges. Though my speech was well enough received by its audience of college administrators, it was not printed in that society's journal. I had disagreed on some points with this eminent benefactor: to publish such disagreement might seem ungrateful—or, more important, possibly, might discourage subsequent largesses from this foundation.

With the interests of certain universities and professors in mind, then, I delete in the following case histories the real names involved; but I have looked into these affairs with some care, and the facts are as I represent them below.

At one state university, the chairman of the department of economics applied to a famous foundation for a sizable grant in support of a departmental research project. In his request, the chairman mentioned that his department believed in an economy of free enterprise. Now although the foundation in question had been established by a most individualistic entrepreneur, the functionaries of the foundation did not seem pleased by this attachment to doctrines shared by the deceased founder. On the contrary, the officers of the foundation informed the applicant for a grant that if his department generally held such views, it was "committed to a point of view," and therefore unworthy of benefaction. But should the chairman see fit to liberalize his department by introducing other opinions, the foundation secretary wrote, then it might be appropriate to apply again for a subsidy; and, indeed, the foundation would be willing to supply the chairman with the names of some promising young scholars whose employment in his department would relieve the monotony of "free enterprise" convictions.

Here the smugness and presumption of one sort of foundation administrator are sufficiently evident. No direct harm was done in this instance: the chairman had simply been admonished to alter his convictions if he wanted money. But sometimes the interference of foundation bureaucrats is more mischievous. The following episode is part of the history of the same foundation as that described above.

At a well-known private university, this big foundation awarded a subsidy to nearly all departments—with the conspicuous exception of the department of political science. Two or three members of this department, well-reputed scholars, were not in the good graces of the foundation. Also the foundation, on making this fat grant to the university, insisted on the appointment of a new administrative vice-president to be nominated by the foundation itself. Under this altered academic regime, the political scientists who had ventured to disagree with the foundation's policies were cast into the outer darkness: one was appointed to a minor post equivalent to the Chiltern Hundreds, and another placed on an extended leave of absence, with the hint that he would do well not to return at all. Eventually, it appears, the department of political science will be favored with a grant—when it is wholly purged of deviant opinions.

Though these are especially disturbing examples of the increasing arrogance of foundations' influence in universities and colleges, a good many others might be cited. Only here and there does one encounter a department or even a university that cannot be bought for a price. And since at present the tendency of the foundation personnel is toward "liberal" social measures, the resistance of faculties to this honeyed interference is less strong than it would be if a big industrial corporation, say, were to make its gifts contingent upon a reform of policy and staff favorable to the corporation's prejudices and interests.

The consequences of large-scale benefaction by foundations upon the whole direction of advanced studies, and even upon undergraduate courses, are almost incalculable. Big subsidies may result in the virtual extinction of certain disciplines or schools of thought, supplanting these by opposing bodies of opinion or academic interests. Perhaps the clearest example of such radical alteration of academic disciplines is the immense growth of "behavioral studies" in political science and sociology, since World War Two. Having determined to back the Behavioralists, foundations like Ford and

Carnegie, in effect, have built enormous patronage empires for the behavioralistic professors, with a corresponding loss of prestige and funds for those scholars who think the study of institutions or of theory should have pride of place over surveys of "behavior." The scholarships and assistantships go, for the most part, to the disciples of the behaviorist persuasion: thus the rising generation of teachers and researchers in such disciplines is indoctrinated in the foundation-favored wing of the social studies.[2]

Because as yet federal grants to higher education have been awarded only incidentally to humane and social studies, it is less easy to point to actions in this realm which affect academic freedom. Among the physical and biological scientists, indeed, there exists already much concern over the increasing domination of the research field by governmental projects. Utilitarian and immediate objectives are favored over pure science and "basic" research, with consequent damage to both research and teaching in the universities. But though in the long run such a domination will touch upon questions of academic freedom, at present the trouble is only in a formative stage.

In those restricted fields of humane and social studies so far subsidized through the National Defense Education Act (NDEA), however, there is more immediate cause for vigilance. Take the language program under the NDEA. The tendency of this project is to favor the rapid development of a shallow competence in language teaching, rather than to reinforce scholarship. The professors influential in such circles are the linguists, rather than the scholars of literature. And the federal funds employed tend to produce a levelling of learning, rewarding the mediocre departments and universities as well as the superior, offering a great number of scholarships—very fat scholarships—with no particular regard for the degree of real culture possessed by the applicants.

These matters bear directly upon academic freedom. The tendency of the federal Office of Education, for instance, has been to award scholarships almost without reference to the grades or judgment of the participating institutions—although the office may

---

[2] See Kirk, "Growing Dangers in 'Campus Research,'" New York *Times Magazine*, Sept. 17, 1961, pp. 22 ff.; also Kirk, "Is Social Science Scientific?" New York *Times Magazine*, June 25, 1961, pp. 11 ff.; and Kirk, "Segments of Political Science Not Amenable to Behavioristic Treatment," in J. C. Charlesworth (ed.), *The Limits of Behavioralism in Political Science* (Philadelphia, 1962), 49–67.

backwater when there are protests from distinguished professors. Also the Office of Education's people lend their authority to projects for producing a multitude of "college language teachers," in a hurry, who in turn will train a greater multitude of highschool language teachers—and to other schemes that produce statistical results fairly promptly and increase the empire of Educationism. The better universities, confronted with a league between inferior institutions and the federal office, grow disheartened; even representatives of long-established state universities hesitate to speak out against aggrandizement of this sort. More and more, decisions in this discipline are made from on high and transmitted to departments of languages which may disagree with the general program, but which comply for the sake of the subsidy.

It is worth noting that my friends in such disciplines, when giving me information, invariably request that their names not be mentioned, should I write about the NDEA language program. When anonymity is sought, even by distinguished scholars, academic freedom is in no prosperous state. Already, when some scholars have ventured in meetings to object to this or that feature of a language scheme, there have been hints by NDEA zealots that Professors X and Y are not "good Americans," or they would go along. Scholars in languages are peculiarly susceptible to this type of intimidation, many of them being foreign-born.

If federal subsidies are extended to the social studies, one may expect a great deal more of this exacting of conformity to grand designs, and more, too, of the struggle for power, along lines vaguely ideological. It is not a matter of direct interference by the White House with the opinions of professors—not at all; rather, the very nature of the centralizing process enables cliques and juntas to exert their will, increasingly, over those academics who tend to their learned knitting instead of pursuing power and novelty.

"Whatever the solution to our pressing educational needs," writes President Douglas Knight, of Duke University, ". . . we must never hand over decisions about the direction of higher education to any one central committee. Centralization in this case might be just as dangerous as incoherence; and we have as much of an obligation to protect the "freedom of indifference" as we do to meet the obvious and enormous needs."[3]

[3] Douglas M. Knight (ed.), *The Federal Government and Higher Education* (Englewood Cliffs, N.J., 1960), 199.

Through long experience, safeguards have been erected, in both state and private educational institutions, to resist pressures hostile to academic freedom from state and local authorities, business and industry, and other outsiders. But there are no present sure guarantees against the novel influence of foundations and of the federal government—the latter always operating from a position of central strength, and the bigger foundations often acting as centralized and centralizing agencies. The illustrations I have offered may suggest that a "central committee" concept of higher education is hostile to the real liberties of the Academy, as Dr. Knight argues. And the "freedom of indifference," which is one of the most valuable possessions of the Academy, has little notion of how to defend itself against these curious new adversaries whose weapon is the open-handed largess.

This writer offers, therefore, some general considerations upon the challenge to academic freedom latent in the growth of foundation subsidy and government subsidy. It is well to look a gift horse in the mouth.

(1) Ideological pressures must accompany these grants-in-aid. Ours is an age of ideology—which I distinguish from political philosophy and principle. From the central government, necessarily, will come demands for professors to be "good Americans"—and not to waste much time in the Ivory Tower. Many foundation staffs are strongly dominated by ideological prejudices—more commonly by what Dr. Sidney Hook calls "ritualistic liberalism" than by anything else. The particular character of the ideological inclination, in both government and foundations, may alter somewhat from decade to decade. But it never will be friendly toward the heirs of Socrates. Latter-day liberals, who at the moment embrace the cause of governmental grants on a grand scale, soon may find themselves the unhappy outsiders.

(2) These grand subsidies will tend to be utilitarian, at the expense of genuinely humane and scientific disciplines. Both the government and the foundations desire results easily tabulated and defensible. Scholars and subjects that do not contribute directly to military defense, "social betterment," or popular appetites will be allowed to wither on the vine.

(3) The administration of these benefactions must be bureaucratic, in the worst sense of that word. The remarkable dullness of the federal Office of Education is admitted by nearly everybody. The

foundations have developed a strange self-perpetuating set of employees, sometimes more interested in their own salaries and their public relations apparatus than in either cultural or material results. (One might demonstrate that, in some instances, the bond joining the managers of certain foundations is a common sense of guilt or inadequacy.) Both bureaucracies tend to resent unusual talents or insubordinate opinions among scholars.

(4) The power of these bureaucracies is more difficult to check or defy than that of other elements which, on occasion, are hostile to academic freedom. Private patrons sometimes were arbitary, true: but while one may discover, without much trouble, another millionaire, one never finds another government. The federal Office of Education and other federal agencies are more remote and conceited than are state legislatures. The great foundations, at once timid and complacent, tend to emulate one another—and what one disapproves, all foundations but a few obdurate little endowments tend to declare anathema. It is most unpleasant for a college or a scholar to be blacklisted by these bureaucracies, unless one has large private means. Diversity has been the principal virtue of the higher learning in America; but these are forces monolithic in character.

If one desires freedom, ordinarily one must make certain sacrifices. If you take the king's shilling, you must fight the king's battles. Most of our colleges and universities already squander a great deal of money upon fads, foibles, and boondoggles; nowadays they are not so desperately in need of more money as they fancy themselves to be.

I am suggesting that, rather than running after governmental and foundational subsidies, the Academy would do well to take such grants only after reflection—and only when certain that the largess is consonant with freedom of teaching and inquiry, calculated to raise the level of humane and scientific disciplines, and to respect the dignity of the scholar. King Stork, after all, was worse than King Log. Harvard University or the University of Chicago, Carleton College or Kenyon or Pomona, or Washington and Lee, will not preserve their virtues when they are suppliants for a dole. And their professors will not preserve their integrity.

An Outsider Looks
at the Catholic College

So far as objectivity is possible in such a matter as this, my observations here are objective. But they are not indifferent, I hope, or unprincipled. "Objectivity" is a word vastly abused nowadays; and it ought not to be employed to suggest a mere disputed middle, or a pretended impartiality that is a mask for strong prejudices. I am writing as a friend to Catholic colleges, but as one who sees them from without, never having been student or regular teacher at any of them.

For some years now, I have been heaping coals of fire upon the heads of the administrators of secular colleges, particularly our larger state institutions. I do know something about such colleges, and I do dare to affirm that they are not what they ought to be. They are what they ought not to be, most of them: degree-mills, custodial institutions for adolescents (Mr. Hutchins' phrase), fortresses of ten-cent-store positivism and nihilism, vocational schools in the grosser sense, institutions that have forgot their ends in the intricacy of their means. I do not deny that there resides some good in them; but many other persons than I are all too eager to sing up that good. My part it seems to be, like that of the prophet Amos whose name I bear, to cry woe unto the city.

The problems of the Catholic colleges nowadays are grave, and to some of their problems there is no answer that can satisfy everyone. The greatest problem, I think, is that of quality versus quantity.

Like all other educational institutions today, the Catholic colleges face the difficulty of a swiftly rising demand for a college education—or at least a college degree—by a multitude much greater, relatively and absolutely, than ever before wanted any such thing. In part, this "rising tide" of enrollments reflects a genuine desire for learning; in much greater part, I think, it reflects only a desire for material preferment and a snob-degree. However this may be, unless there is some profound alteration of opinion and economic circumstance in this nation, all colleges, for years to come, will be beseiged by young people—and the young people's parents—who are intent upon crowding their way into the Academy. And the Catholic colleges—more severely than the state institutions, more seriously even than the Protestant denominational colleges and the secular private colleges—are perplexed by the question of how wide their doors ought to be opened. This problem is more sobering for the Catholic colleges than for the secular institutions and the Protestant colleges, because Catholic colleges are a means for leavening the dough of modern thought and society; they are a conscious defense of Christian faith—and that the faith of a conscious minority—in a time given over to will and appetite. I need not labor this point. The Catholic colleges desire to receive as many students as they can, that they may counter the secularism and positivism and nihilism that oppress this age and that are strong in most other institutions of learning. They are right to do so; they are a bulwark of truth and order among us. It is not too much to say that the Catholic colleges snatch brands from the burning; and how hot

that modern fire is at many non-Catholic colleges I know better than
many other people, perhaps. The average priest-teacher or brother-
teacher and even the average lay-teacher in Catholic colleges rarely
is indulged in a clear glimpse of the rationalistic and mechanistic
and ideological opinions still dominant at so many other institutions.
"Under certain conditions that are already partly in sight," Irving
Babbitt wrote some forty years ago, "the Catholic Church may
perhaps be the only institution left in the Occident that can be
counted on to uphold civilized standards." Nowadays those conditions are wholly in sight.

But the problem is not simply one of what the Catholic colleges
would like to do; it is one of what they *can* do, given their limited
resources. Theirs must be a prudential judgment. It scarcely seems
necessary to say that the Catholic colleges are short of money; and
the odds are that they never will have half enough money. As things
are going, they will be fortunate if, like Alice, they can keep running
as fast as they can in order to stay where they are. The average
Catholic layman is more prosperous, relatively, than were his immediate ancestors in this country; but the increasing burden of federal,
state, and local taxation—the taxation which, among other things,
pays for the immense expansion of the secular institutions—already
consumes much of what money might have gone to Catholic
colleges, and may consume more in future. Most of the great tax-
exempt foundations exhibit no marked cordiality toward the Catholic colleges. The Catholic colleges, I fear, simply will not be able to
increase infinitely in size or number and at the same time to improve,
or even maintain, their standards of scholarship. They will have to
make a hard choice, I suspect; to give a great mass of students a
mediocre training in almost everything, or to give a tolerable number of select students a decent education in certain established
disciplines.

I do not mean to cast the former alternative aside contemptuously: I know the powerful arguments which support such a
choice, and even sympathize with those who employ them. It is hard
and sometimes dangerous to decline a mission to the masses; and it is
the duty of Catholic colleges to educate as many young people as
they reasonably can. Yet, the means being limited, I am inclined to
believe that the Catholic colleges would be wiser to choose the latter
alternative, that of giving a tolerable number of select students a
decent education.

In short, to Catholic colleges I recommend quality over quantity; and that upon the hard ground of necessity, without embarking upon higher arguments. For in quantity, the Catholic colleges have lost the battle already; they never will be able to enroll one tenth as many students as do the secular institutions. Nor is it probable that many Catholic colleges will be able to afford, much longer, the costly race in "plant," "amenities," and "special facilities"—not if they also are intent upon vastly increased enrollment. The stadiums, the big student lounges, the elaborate engineering workshops, the enormous apparatus of vocational and quasi-vocational training—for all this the secular institution, if not the Protestant colleges, always will have much more money; and in such things, the Catholic colleges, at best—with a few exceptions—will be merely "almost as good" as their rivals. To be almost as good, in any field of endeavor, is to join the vanquished. And in all the devices of amusement and catch-courses that are intended to lure the mass-student of the new age, the Catholic colleges always will be handicapped, in conscience and in funds. In such matters, the popular techniques of enrollment building are hopelessly costly to the Catholic college.

And even if, abjuring the frivolities and ostentations of modern higher learning, the Catholic colleges should endeavor merely to increase enrollments markedly in traditional and less expensive disciplines, still here they would be unwise to embark upon a quantity competition with the secular universities and colleges, I think. For, in the long run, the influence of educational establishments is measured not by how many graduates they turn out, but by the mental and moral fibre of those graduates. Princeton, for instance, always will count for more than Behemoth State College, even though Behemoth, year upon year, has ten times the enrollment of Princeton. The Catholic colleges cannot hope to equal Behemoth in enrollment, in any event; but they may justly aspire to establish a reputation and an influence like that of Princeton, for instance.

The Catholic faith, it seems to me, and the interest of all Christians, and of all our civilization, will be better served today by a reputation for intellectual power and moral worth than by mere numbers. Any folly or fallacy can attract numbers. But in the long run, intelligence will tell, even in a university. More than anything else, what Christian faith and Christian learning require today is a restoration of their intellectual respectability and their moral efficacy. If that reputation is restored, the influence upon the masses—and upon secular institutions—will follow. It will not then be necessary to compete with Behemoth State in numbers; for Behemoth State, even, in some degree, will be converted by example.

The task of restoring the reputation of Christian faith and learning—and that of Catholic colleges—is terribly urgent. Monsignor John Tracy Ellis has not exaggerated the frequent public doubt of the intellectual respectability and moral efficacy of Catholic colleges—whether or not that public impression really is justified. A soft impeachment admitted by the friends of Catholic educational establishments becomes, in the mouth of the ideologue and the secularistic zealot, a fierce defamation. Even if the Catholic colleges are no worse than other colleges—and I think they are not worse, but in some things perceptibly better—still they must become *conspicuously* better than other colleges, in a good many things, if they are to restore the reputation of Christian faith and learning in this time; for they labor under a handicap of prejudice.

And there are certain outward signs, whether or not these are just indices, that tell against the Catholic colleges nowadays. One is the frequent omission of *any* Catholic college from published lists of the better colleges in the United States. One of the better surveys of this sort was that of the Chicago *Tribune* which appeared about a decade ago. I had a hand myself in that survey, and I happened to list some Catholic universities and colleges in the several categories considered. My choices appear, however, not to have been the choices of the other persons consulted by the *Tribune*. This omission of the Catholic institutions is not to be attributed primarily to any no-Popery feeling. Rather, it results I think from the fact that very few scholars and journalists, outside the Catholic educational realm, really know much about the Catholic colleges, for good or ill; and we can commend only those institutions with which we happen to be acquainted. There is probably no remedy for this condition, except to make some Catholic colleges so *conspicuously* good that they cannot be ignored by any well-meaning non-Catholic scholar or journalist.

Another outward sign that tells against the Catholic colleges, as representatives of intellectual power, is the paucity of Catholic students and professors in the lists of persons awarded competitive fellowships and scholarships—in the Fulbright program, for instance. This fact has been remarked upon by the editors of *America,* among others. In this matter, I have some reason to believe, there does operate something of the old no-Popery spirit, even if only in a vague and half-repressed sense: the mutter of "Remember, remember, the Fifth of November, Guy Fawkes and the Gunpowder Plot." I am suspicious of such questions, on some application blanks for certain competitive fellowships, as this: "Is the candidate, in your opinion, a representative American?" I don't know what a representative American is; and if I did know, I doubt that representative Americans ought to be chosen—exceptional Americans would be better. But I harbor a glimmering surmise that just possibly in the minds of the authors of such questions, and all too possibly in the minds of many professors who answer such questions, a Catholic is not a representative American. Such prejudices are fairly strong in a number of great charitable foundations, and perhaps dominant in certain professorial quarters. The whole subject would bear a closer inquiry. Here I suggest only that such prejudices are not extinct, and that the most efficacious way to counter them is to make Catholic colleges undeniably strong in intellectual repute. To be merely "just as good" or "almost as good" as other colleges will not do at all; only remarkable probity overcomes prejudice.

A third outward sign that tells against the Catholic colleges, in public opinion, is what I may call a certain intellectual naivete not infrequent among Catholic students, whether enrolled in Catholic or in secular colleges. One form of this naivete is an unbookishness, an intellectual sluggishness, which in considerable part may be explained historically by the peculiar handicaps of occupation, class, and economic status under which American Catholicism has long labored: young people from unlettered households do not become fine scholars overnight. This particular handicap is gradually being reduced by the improved status of American Catholic families; but meanwhile it impairs the reputation of Catholic colleges in some degree. (And I may add here that, so far as the performance of schools goes, the average students from Catholic schools are better prepared for college work than the average students from public schools.) If we deny a fact, however, that fact will become our master. One of the best ways for overcoming this variety of intellectual naivete, and the general reputation it brings, is to make the Catholic colleges conspicuous for intellectual discipline and aspiration.

There is a second form of intellectual naivete: a certain smugness to be discerned even among the better Catholic students. Cardinal Newman might have called this attitude provinciality; and in some degree it be a mark of what some eminent American Catholics have called the "Catholic ghetto-mentality." One facet of this smugness is a naive and uncritical employment of Scholastic doctrines in every argument or exigency. The restoration of the Schoolmen's right reason is one of the grand achievements of twentieth-century Catholic education in America; but even the Scholastic method can be carried to excess. A professor at a Catholic university writes to me of his interesting endeavor to teach Newman to undergraduates: "It has been a bit difficult, because my students are scholastically grounded, and, to quote Newman's quotation of St. Ambrose, it did not please God to save His people by logic." The recourse to authority is one of the virtues of Catholic education; yet there are problems not solved and heights not attained by the simple citing of a syllogism. I suggest here only that Catholic colleges, if they are to establish enduring reputations, must be catholic in learning.

There is one more outward sign I would like to discuss which tells against the Catholic college. I remarked earlier that what Christian faith and Christian learning need today is a restoration of their reputation for intellectual strength and moral effectiveness. My final point, though it may seem trifling, touches upon moral efficacy, one of the proofs of the genuineness of belief. Works cannot be ignored by the Catholic. But does a Catholic higher education seem to work toward moral efficacy? On one point, at least, there is reason for doubt; and it is a disagreeable little point.

I refer to the problem, or rather the curse, of cheating in college examinations. This vice has grown much worse in America in recent years, one of many symptoms of the decay of a sense of honor and duty. (Cheating of this sort is also, of course, a mark of puerility, for the cheat is himself the cheated, in the long run.) It pervades most colleges. And Catholic colleges are not exempted; indeed, several friends of mine who have taught in both Catholic and secular colleges inform me that the frequency of this offense is greater in Catholic colleges. (I cannot vouch for this myself; I can only say that among students at secular institutions, the Catholics seem no worse—and no better—in this respect than the other students, so far as I have been able to gauge.)

Why this is so—*if* it is so—I can only guess. Some critics of Catholic education might maintain that such conduct is the product of a faulty understanding of the function of contrition and absolution. Others might argue that this suggests the superiority of private conscience, as a moral agent, over authority. These, however, are not my views. I incline toward an historical explanation, if the thing be true at all. I think of the story of the Irishman, just landed in America, who demanded, "What's the government in this country? and I'm agin it." If one's immediate forebears took it for a positive virtue to evade the decrees of London or St. Petersburg or Naples, it is easy for one to slip into the habit of evading the powers that be in a college administration. Orestes Brownson, by the way, was well aware of the difficulties this "agin the government" attitude created among American Catholics. But perhaps I digress.

My purpose in raising this small and disagreeable topic is to suggest that there is something disquieting about students who read—and recite from—St. Thomas Aquinas' *On Truth* and then proceed to copy someone else's test paper. I propose no simple remedies. I merely suggest that such problems as these will be aggravated by an increase in enrollments. For deception is easier in a crowd, and shamefaced—or barefaced—anonymity comes with the herd. Once a college enrollment exceeds a tolerably humane scale, the vices of a mob begin to work: I have seen the thing happen. And while the secular institution may not profess much concern for moral efficacy, the Catholic college must.

My theme, in fine, is this: it seems that if the Catholic college must make the choice between quality and quantity, it ought to choose quality for the sake not simply of scholarship, but for the defense, the effectual defense, of Christian faith and Christian learning. To high reputation in the liberal arts and the pure sciences, Catholic colleges have a clear road: for very few other colleges are treading that path. This is a noble opportunity. In the fullness of time, it is the theological and humane and scientific disciplines which will tell, not today's football victories and technological displays. A leanness of means actually may result in an amplitude of ends.

"What we want," Orestes Brownson wrote in 1873, "is a high-toned Catholic public opinion, independent of the public opinion of the country at large, and in strict accordance with Catholic tradition and Catholic aspirations." Brownson saw even then the beginnings of such a Catholic public opinion in the young men issuing from the Catholic colleges. For my part, I hope that the Catholic colleges will continue to produce a high-toned Catholic public opinion and will not waste their energies in a material race with institutions whose material resources are infinitely greater. I hope that Catholic colleges, like Catholic public opinion, will remain independent of the public opinion of the country at large. If they do, they may succeed, after some years or decades, in working a beneficent restoration of American colleges and American public opinion at large.

American Colleges: A Proposal for Reform

*T*he sound statesman, as Edmund Burke once said, combines a disposition to preserve with an ability to reform. So, I hope, does the better educator. American colleges are worth preserving; but they can be preserved, in our time of flux, only if they are reformed. I propose to suggest here the lineaments of a conservative reform. Perhaps I should call it a restoration, rather than a reform; for what I have in mind is a return to the original purposes and functions of American colleges.

Prudent change is the means for conserving the continuity of any institution. Whether that prudent change ought to be "forward" in a bold new direction, or "backward," to a restoration of old essentials neglected, depends upon particular circumstances and the temper of the age. In general, our age seems to require a reform that is reactionary, rather than innovating; for while there is slight risk that our generation may cease suddenly to invent new things, there is grave risk that our generation may break the contract of eternal society, forgetting that we are wise in our generation only because our modern intellectual edifices rest upon ancient foundations, the moral and intellectual achievements of our ancestors.

So I am proposing a prudent restoration of the ends and means of higher education in American colleges—a reactionary reform, if you will. I feel that American colleges must retrace their steps, or perish. The possibility of extinction is not remote. Various persons predict, some with regret, some with a tone resembling elation, that one fourth or more of our liberal arts colleges may cease to be within a decade. I think that some of these estimates are high; but undeniably a great many of the several hundred old-fashioned American colleges are experiencing hard sledding, and every year that passes is marked by the disappearance of a number of colleges. I mean, of course, those characteristically American foundations we call liberal arts colleges, not our universities or technical institutes or agricultural colleges or teachers' colleges. No state-supported educational establishments are going by the board; on the contrary, nearly all of them are unhealthily swollen in enrollments and lavishly supported by state funds. Nor are many of our older private universities in straitened circumstances, though some are feeling the pinch—Johns Hopkins and Stanford among them—and even Harvard and Chicago complain that their endowments are inadequate for meeting present necessities. I am concerned here with America's especial contribution to higher education, the college of liberal arts and sciences, governed by a private board of trustees, ordinarily limited in enrollment to a few hundred students, and concerned with the schooling of undergraduates in the traditional intellectual disciplines which train the liberal understanding and prepare young people for the life of reason. And those colleges, most of them, have fallen upon evil days.

This situation is sufficiently paradoxical, for no other nation spends so much upon higher education, per head of population, as does America; and never before has so large a proportion of the population of any country attended colleges and universities. The state-supported institutions are swamped by "the rising tide" of enrollments; and, for that matter, many of the liberal arts colleges enroll twice as many students as they did before the war. Yet in a time when the desire for a college degree, as social distinction and as means to economic advantage, is more general than ever before, the majority of private colleges find themselves lacking in funds and lacking in able students. Whatever is the matter?

A part of the difficulty is financial. The general inflation which this country has experienced since 1940 has cut in half the purchasing power of college revenues derived from fixed endowments, except when those endowments have been invested in enterprises whose profits have risen proportionately. At the same time, income taxes and inheritance taxes have considerably diminished gifts and legacies to colleges, except so far as partial exemption from taxation has encouraged some new beneficiaries to contribute to charitable and educational causes. But the millionaire patron of the college now is a very rare bird. I shall not advance any simple, direct remedy for this condition, except to suggest that if the colleges really were considered important by the public, sufficient money would be forthcoming somehow.

Another cause of the difficulty is the ascendancy of state-supported institutions. Formerly private colleges constituted the great majority in our roster of educational institutions; now slightly less than half the total number of college students in the country is enrolled in private colleges. In one or two states, there are no private colleges at all; in the growing industrial state of Michigan, only about 18 percent of the students are enrolled in private institutions of higher learning. As it has grown progressively more difficult for private colleges to obtain sufficient funds, it has grown progressively less difficult for state-supported institutions to obtain legislative appropriations. Thus the state institutions are able to afford the expensive buildings, the high salaries, the athletic fields and stadiums and swimming pools, the student-union buildings, the public relations departments, the recruitment campaigns, the triumphant football teams, and the name-band dances, which are the outward —but only the outward—signs of an educational institution which, the public thinks, is going places. Most private colleges simply are unable to compete in any appreciable degree with these trappings. Again, I do not intend here to suggest any simple solution for this particular difficulty; I venture only to murmur that to hold its own against these material attractions, the liberal arts college must offer something different in kind.

Now a third cause of the colleges' plight, and that cause much more pernicious than the previous two reasons for their distress, is the private colleges' failure to fulfill their own original purposes, to adhere to their own established methods, and to provide an education different in kind from that offered by the state-supported institutions. I do not mean that all the liberal arts colleges have been false to their traditions. At Haverford, Williams, Washington and Lee, Kenyon, the University of the South, Reed, Wesleyan, Mount Holyoke, and perhaps a score of other famous colleges, you will find the old curriculum and the old standards, at least, still rather closely adhered to, whatever may be said concerning fidelity to the moral and social principles of the founders of some of these institutions. Such colleges still respect the works of the mind and still produce a number of graduates who are genuinely educated persons. They are likely to endure, whatever happens to the bulk of the colleges in this country, because for the most part they fulfill their old function and are respected and supported accordingly. (Though even some of these feel the ground trembling underfoot.) But most colleges are now in a precarious situation because they do not profess anything not professed by the state-supported institutions, and because they do not provide any advantages to faculty, students, and the public which are not more than offset by the advantages of their rivals in the realm of higher education. Their failure, in short, is a punishment for a dereliction in duty.

A representative of a charitable foundation, accustomed to visiting a great many college campuses in the course of a year, recently observed to me that any college which believes in anything still is in a state comparatively healthy—and sometimes thriving—no matter how sound or how silly its belief may be. If that college clearly has faith in orthodox Christianity, or in militant atheism, or in old-fangled *laissez faire*, or in revisionist socialism, or in some ancient discipline of the mind, or in some startling intellectual departure, then that college does not lack for a vigorous faculty, or a lively student body, or a generous group of patrons. Commitment to principle brings success as a by-product. And my own desultory visits to some scores of campuses tend to confirm the argument of this foundation representative.

But most colleges are terrified of commitment to principle; indeed, they are opposed to principles on principle. Their trustees and presidents and faculty members tend to think of doubt as a good in itself, of ambivalence as identical with the liberal understanding, and of faith as bigotry. Thus they are left only with quantitative standards, or, at best, a vague aestheticism, for their rudder in this sea of troubles.

The state-supported institutions always can trounce the private colleges where quantitative standards are concerned; while as for aestheticism, art itself is froth when divorced from purposes and norms. If the colleges will not commit themselves to any principles, it is scarcely surprising that the public will not commit its education to the colleges. Weigh an institution with no standards and no stadium against an institution with no standards and a great massive stadium; well, it is no wonder that the balance swings to the state-supported institutions. Men of considerable intelligence and large means sometimes ask me why they should send their sons to small colleges, as against state universities, when the colleges no longer seem to stand for anything in particular; officers of charitable foundations sometimes ask me why they should expend funds upon small colleges with no particular reason for existence, when the famous professors and the great laboratories are at Behemoth University. And though I am a humble friend to the liberal arts colleges, I am unable to advance any very weighty argument in their favor, granted the dereliction from duty upon which I have touched.

But a very powerful defense of the liberal arts colleges can be made, if these colleges return to the performance of their old duties; and if, indeed, they resume their original functions, they will not require much apology from their well-wishers. For I think that the particular conditions of our century and our society demand now, more than ever before, a restoration of liberal learning. The hour is favorable to the colleges, if only the people who control college policy can perceive their present opportunity.

Although the American college derived its purposes and disciplines from a very old European scheme of education and was particularly influenced in its beginnings by the colleges of Oxford and Cambridge, it became, as it developed, a unique institution. Small, often secluded, and primarily a foundation for teaching rather than for the maintenance of finished scholars, it soon

influenced the whole tone and temper of American life: the direct
effect of Harvard and Yale in New England, or William and Mary in
Virginia, upon the life of the mind and the conduct of society can
scarcely be paralleled in any country or era. When the university,
well into the nineteenth century, began to develop in the United
States, it took the German system for its model; and until quite
recent years, at least, the university in America has not affected the
life and leadership of the nation so profoundly as has the college. If
the liberal arts college ceases to be, the root of much in American
culture will have been destroyed.

Now the aim of the old-fangled college education was ethical, the
development of moral understanding and humane leadership; but
the method was intellectual, the training of mind and conscience
through well-defined literary disciplines. A college was an establishment for the study of literature: it is nearly that simple. Through an
apprehension of great literature young men were expected to fit
themselves for leadership in the churches, in politics, in law, in the
principal positions of community responsibility. This was what the
late Gordon Chalmers (after Sir Thomas Elyot) called "the education of governors." Whatever the faults of this system, it did produce
a body of high-principled and literate men to be the leaders of the
American democracy. They learned to govern themselves and to
serve the republic, through strict attention to great literature: the
poetry, philosophy, and history of Greece and Rome, especially; the
Bible, with Hebrew history; something of modern thought and
languages; and something of the literature of science. The subjects
of study were few, and the course of study was uniform. The
intention of the college was not to confer a vague smattering of every
branch of knowledge upon its students, but rather to teach them the
fundamental disciplines of logical thought, provide them with a
taste and critical faculty for independent reading, and then send
them into the world with a cast of character and mind fitted for
ethical and intellectual leadership. If these young men remembered
no more from college than something of Biblical history and
precepts from Cicero and episodes from Plutarch—and some young
men retained a great deal besides—still that knowledge prepared
them better for life, the life of their age or of ours, than does the
cafeteria-curriculum of many universities and colleges nowadays,
whose graduates may read not a single important book after they
have got their diplomas.

If an institution of higher learning could confer upon its students the sort of liberal education described by Newman, many of the problems of modern society might be solved in short order. But to expect such a general achievement is to set our sights impossibly high, in this day and age. We shall be fortunate if we manage to restore in our time a standard of achievement roughly equivalent to that attained by the old-fangled American college, which at its best fell considerably short of Newman's ideal. I am not arguing for a reform which promises to give us a nation of scholars and gentlemen, but only for a reform which may leaven the lump of modern American society with a sprinkling of men and women who know what it is to be truly human, who have some taste for contemplation, who take long views, and who have a sense of moral responsibility and intellectual order. That goal, though difficult to reach, is not beyond our powers.

Most surviving American colleges fail to achieve this fairly modest goal because they try to be all things to all men. They promise what they cannot perform, and never could perform. They promise to teach adjustment to the group, sociability, trades, salesmanship, business acumen, and the art of worldly wisdom. They ape the functions of the universities and the technical schools. With murmured apology and shame-facedness they consign their old disciplines to a dusty corner of the curriculum—when they do not abolish the classics, polite letters, languages, moral philosophy, and speculative science altogether. Business science, communications skill, journalism, and pre-medicine usurp the arts which teach us what it is to be a man. Most of the colleges have abandoned their ethical end and forgotten their intellectual means. The wonder is not that the colleges are in difficulties, but that they survive at all. For when function ceases, form atrophies.

Certain things a good college can do very well. It can give the student the tools for educating himself throughout his life. It can present to him certain general principles for the governance of personality and community. It can help him to see what makes life worth living. It can teach him basic disciplines which will be of infinite value to him in professional specialization at a university, or in his subsequent apprenticeship to any commercial or industrial occupation. And certain things no honest college can pretend to do at all. It cannot teach him directly how to win friends and influence people. It cannot make him a successful captain of industry, or an engineer, or a specialized scientist. It cannot guarantee him worldly prosperity. It cannot simply enroll him in a "survey course in world culture" and pour wisdom into him, as milk is poured into a bottle.

Now it is quite possible that a person who has been immersed in the pseudo-schooling and vocational courses of a corrupted college may enjoy a considerable measure of practical success, and at the same time be an intelligent and honest man. Two friends of mine, who attended the same college as I did, there majored in journalism. One can no more really learn the trade of journalism in college than one can really learn the craft of whaling from reading *Moby Dick*. One may acquire in college, indeed, a knowledge of what current events mean from courses in history. But "majoring in journalism" has nothing to do with this. My two friends, despite their college curriculum, read good books and fill responsible positions: one is chief project engineer of an important automobile factory, and the other is chief underwriter of a state workmen's compensation fund. They redeemed themselves from the faults of their formal education, and, for that matter, learned a good deal during their college years—but not from the vocational training they had fondly embraced. My moral, of course, is this: the good to be got from college is what the late Albert Jay Nock called the "useless knowledge" absorbed there—a body of knowledge commonly forgotten in detail, but infinitely valuable as discipline and residue. The useful knowledge, the practical instruction, is obsolete almost before the student enters the practical world. A college is wasting its students' time and its own resources when it pretends to teach what can really be taught only in workaday life, in the graduate school, or in the trade school.

What the college really ought to do, and we can do, was expressed succinctly by Irving Babbitt in a book published half a century ago, *Literature and the American College*. (The study of literature, I repeat, is the primary instrument of college education; and when British universities consider introducing a new course of study, they still put to themselves this essential question, "To what body of literature does the proposed course of study refer?") Babbitt, then, was not writing merely of courses in the poetry of Keats and Shelley when he gave his enduring little book its title. He wrote:

"The best of the small colleges will render a service to American education if they decide to make a sturdy defense of the humane tradition instead of trying to rival the great universities in displaying a full line of educational novelties. In the latter case, they may become third-rate and badly equipped scientific schools, and so reenact the fable of the frog that tried to swell itself to the size of an ox. . . . Even though the whole world seem bent on living the quantitative life, the college should remember that its business is to make of its graduates men of quality in the real and not the conventional meaning of the term. In this way it will do its share toward creating that aristocracy of character and intelligence which is needed in a community like ours to take the place of an aristocracy of birth, and to counteract the tendency toward an aristocracy of money."

Throughout the past fifty years, the average American college has disregarded Babbitt's admonition, pleading that the college must give the public what the public demanded. But now the time is upon us when the college can and must return to the principles which Babbitt himself so well exemplified. The great state-supported institutions have so thoroughly yielded to the presumed "public demand" for specialization, vocationalism, and intellectual egalitarianism that even the most complaisant liberal arts college can no longer successfully compete with its vast subsidized rivals for the favors of the students who desire, or think they desire, a shallow veneer of "culture," a trade-school discipline with a college diploma, and four years of idleness. If the private college competes with the state-supported institution along such lines, the private college will succeed in enrolling only those students who fail to meet even the lax academic requirements of the state-supported institutions. And no one is going to be much interested in keeping alive a college which has become not much better than an intellectual bargain-basement stuffed with rejects from the upper floors.

The public demand now seems to be shifting from an emphasis upon narrow vocational schooling and "training for success" to a desire—as yet somewhat vaguely expressed—for liberal knowledge and cultivation of general aptitudes. In industry, in business, and in governmental service there has been felt a pressing need for men and women who know something of human nature, of history, of imaginative literature, of science in its larger meanings. The unpleasant necessity encountered by many industries for wholly retraining college graduates who had majored in chemical engineering, public relations, personnel management, or business administration has had something to do with this change of temper. The chief engineer of a great manufacturing company not long ago remarked to a friend of mine that he had found only one engineer under his jurisdiction, in all his years with the company, who both "knew, and knew how to write about it"—and that man he had imported from England. Even in the age of automation—or, perhaps, especially in the age of automation—the young person really prepared for life and work is the person who has been schooled in the humane disciplines.

With reference to this age of automation, Mr. Peter Drucker wrote once that our colleges ought not to feel that they now need to lower standards in order to attract students and thus survive. For as things are going, we shall have many more prospective college students than can possibly be enrolled anywhere. It is the college which can boast of its high standards, its exclusiveness, that will attract the better students and the benefactions of industry, the foundations, and the private patron. The college can survive not by imitating the mass-education methods of Brummagem University, but by offering a discipline of intellect, ethical in purpose, which mass education neglects. A return to original function, in short, is becoming the first law of self-preservation for the private college.

So I venture here to set down, tentatively, some general rules by which the prudent college might be guided in its work of conservative reform. To undertake them would require some courage of the people responsible for a college's policies; and the success of such a reform would be dependent, in part, upon what Professor Arthur Bestor calls "the restoration of learning" in our primary and secondary schools and upon certain readjustments in the graduate schools of our universities. But one has to begin somewhere; the American college cannot afford much longer to drift with the current of events; and out of urgent necessity, if from no higher motive, the college policy-makers may begin to reexamine the ends and means of a college education.

1. The college should reaffirm that the end of a liberal education is an ethical consciousness, through which the student is brought to an apprehension of the enduring truths which govern our being, the principles of self-control, and the dignity of man.

2. The college should make it clear that this ethical end is sought through an intellectual discipline, exacting in its character, which regards "useless knowledge" as infinitely more valuable than simple utilitarian skills.

3. The college should return to a concise curriculum emphasizing classical literature, languages, moral philosophy, history, the pure

sciences, logic, rhetoric, and religious knowledge.

4. The college should set its face against amorphous "survey courses," "general education," and similar substitutes for real intellectual discipline: such a smattering of an inchoate mass of fact produces only the little learning which is a dangerous thing.

5. The college should turn away from vocationalism, resigning to trade schools and industrial "in-service" training programs what the college never was meant to undertake.

6. The college should abandon its attempt to encroach upon the specialized and professional studies which are the proper province of the graduate schools of universities.

7. The college should say less about "socialization" and "personality-building" and more about the improvement of the human reason, for the human reason's own sake.

8. The smaller college should give up as lost endeavor its aspiration to attract those students who desire the "extra-curricular activities" of Behemoth University, and offer instead its own natural advantages of personal relationships, smallness of scale, and respect for individuality.

9. The college should not content itself with enrolling those students who cannot obtain admittance to a great university or state college; on the contrary, it should begin to set its standards higher than those of Behemoth University.

10. The college should endeavor deliberately to keep its student body within reasonable limits, its humane scale being one of its principal natural advantages over Behemoth University.

11. The college should emancipate itself from quasi-commercialized programs of athletics, an expensive and often anti-intellectual pastime in which it cannot compete successfully with Behemoth University.

12. The college should reduce to a minimum the elective feature in its curriculum; for one of the college's principal virtues is its recognition of order and hierarchy in the higher learning, and the undergraduate ordinarily is not yet capable of judging with discretion what his course of studies ought to be.

13. The college should recall the importance of furnishing society with a body of tolerably well-educated persons whose function it is to provide right reason and conscience in the commonwealth.

14. The college should inculcate in its students a sense of diffuse gratitude toward the generations that have preceded us in time, and

a sense of obligation toward the generations yet to be born; it should remind the rising generation that we are part of a great continuity and essence, and that we moderns are only dwarfs mounted upon the shoulders of giants. For this consciousness lies at the heart of a liberal education.

Can We
Apprehend Science?

Are most educated people nowadays grossly ignorant of the physical and natural sciences? If they are ignorant, does this matter? And if that does matter, what can we do by way of remedy? Discussion of such subjects has flourished these past three years and more—but often the debate has been superficial in character, perhaps because of the shallowness of the Rede Lectures by C. P. Snow (now Sir Charles Snow) that opened the argument.

I essay, then, three tasks: first, to suggest that ignorance of scientific disciplines and terminology, though regrettable, is not so general nor so profound as some people declare it to be; second, to argue that though this ignorance raises problems, the real difficulties are not those advanced by Snow and his set; third, to offer recommendations for alleviating the disturbing conditions.

In order to know anything, said John Henry Newman, we must resign ourselves to ignorance of much. The imperial intellects of old—Aristotle, Aquinas, Bacon, Pascal—more nearly comprehended the body of learning of their times than can the modern scholars; yet we ought not to think even of these men of genius as walking encyclopedias. Where technique, rather than first principles, is in question, the philosopher never has been omniscient: Aristotle presumably would have cut a poor figure had he endeavored to compound cosmetics for Greek ladies (chemistry being, among the Greeks, the province of base mechanicals, not scientists); and Bacon might have failed as master of a tanyard.

So it is vain to reproach the leaders and decision-makers of modern society for having an imperfect command of the immense body of modern technology. If, in medieval times, every guild craft was a "mystery" beyond the ken of prince and priest, surely one need not marvel that the vastly more complex applications of modern science have not been mastered by politicians, men of letters, and moulders of public opinion. Since the worker in one realm of technology usually is ignorant enough of the skills in another field of applied science, one can hardly expect men of humane and social disciplines to judge authoritatively in matters of engineering, industrial production technique, or new armaments. Richard I did not have leisure enough to experiment with the forging of Damascus blades; and President Charles de Gaulle had other concerns than the relative merits of particular testing devices of the French atomic research staff. No way ever existed to crowd into the brief span of human life an acquaintance with all skills—even though Peter the Great essayed this—and no such way ever can be attained. Where technique is in question, the leaders of society—let alone most of us—must rely upon general principles, expert advice, and examination of practical consequences.

A quick and penetrating intellect, indeed, may grasp sufficiently a particular technique, in case of need, by intense though abrupt application—supposing that intellect to have been grounded previously in both scientific approaches and in the exercise of the higher imagination. Emphasis upon genuine education—upon systematic development of the intellectual faculties—rather than the vain endeavor to burden the brain with a crushing load of facts about myriad techniques, offers us our chief hope for governing competently our modern scientific and industrial and technological upheaval. Mere technical training cannot suffice; yet the union of humane learning with scientific methodology remains within the limits of possibility.

Sir Charles Snow, however, laments that "the literary intellectuals," political leaders, and most other folk have not come to terms with the industrial revolution and modern technology. While this reproach might have been just a century ago, its ring is curiously archaic in 1965. Even before the middle of the nineteenth century, the masters of the state were abandoning the old political and moral disciplines in favor of preoccupation with utilitarian concerns: Chateaubriand, after commenting upon the far-ranging talents of seventeenth-century statists, concluded, "But nowadays the statesman understands only the stock-market—and that badly." In 1965, there exists little peril that the man at the top, or the man in the street, will pay too little heed to the latest gadgets; on the contrary, what they neglect is wisdom, including the art of worldly wisdom. Limitless enthusiasm has been generated for putting a man on the moon, but only obdurate gadflies still ask, "To what end?"

If, nevertheless, men are projected to the moon, or if diesel-powered ships are supplanted by atomic-driven vessels, certainly our makers of decisions must know something of the character of these changes and of the means for controlling or directing them; our critics of ideas and our imaginative writers cannot well leave technological change out of account. It is much to be desired that twentieth-century statesmen emulate John Quincy Adams or Lord Salisbury in their lively understanding of scientific progress; it is even to be wished that men of letters might share Tennyson's interest in industrial innovation.[1] Truly things are in the saddle in our era,

---

[1] But one cannot expect the poet ever to become a technical expert; the poet, too, must give primacy to his own art. When, after his first railway ride, Tennyson wrote of "the ringing grooves of change," he labored under the illusion that the wheels of the locomotive and carriages ran within flanged grooves. To have sacrificed *The Passing of Arthur* to a greater mastery of technological detail would scarcely have brought closer even that bourgeois egalitarian future so smugly commended by Sir Charles Snow, middlebrow naturalistic novelist.

and if mankind is not to be ridden by its own machines, the higher imagination must concern itself, in part, with the giant computing machine and the cobalt bomb.

Technology being the bastard child of pure science, a parental resumption of interest in this natural offspring may be obtained through application to scientific principle by our men of intellect and will—though the brat cannot be chastened by science alone. In fine, I am all for really scientific understanding and the improvement of the teaching of science in our educational establishment.

Nor is this imparting of true science to a great many people—including "literary intellectuals" and politicians—a fantastic aspiration. The dimming of nineteenth-century hopes for a reconstruction of human nature and society through application to scientific doctrines and techniques ought not to cast us into the opposite error of considering the average intellect hopelessly impervious to science. Brougham aspired to exorcise, through popularized science, the "evil spirits of tyranny and persecution which haunted the long night now gone down the sky"; Sir Robert Peel declared that knowledge of physical science would confer upon the dying "pleasure and consolation." This rodomontage of vulgarized scientism has gone down the way to dusty death in company with Victorian meliorism generally—or should have, though it still echoes on the lips of this or that zealot for the Empire of Science. But the abandonment of Utopian claims need not deter us from imparting to reasonably intelligent people the rudiments of scientific discipline—and with such knowledge, the possibility of putting man back into the saddle.

Let me observe, parenthetically, that I am very well aware of the difficulty of persuading people of a poetic or historical cast of mind to address themselves to the natural and physical sciences—for it is my own difficulty. To read Aquinas is as hard for me as it is pleasurable to read Dante; to study Newton is a chore, though to keep company with Swift is a delight. Nor am I suggesting that we can cure all the ills to which flesh is heir by making the masses scientifically minded. Rather, in Newman's words, "The heart is commonly reached, not through the reason, but through the imagination, by means of direct impressions, by the testimony of facts and events, by history, by description. Persons influence us, voices melt us, looks subdue us, deeds inflame us. Many a man will live and die upon a dogma: no man will be a martyr for a conclusion." These reservations notwithstanding, application to genuine science is possible for nearly all reasonably endowed minds, if the disciplines are imparted soon enough; and the gulf between "the two cultures," scientific and humane, is not yet unbridgeable. William Butler Yeats—so detested by Sir Charles Snow—was more capable than are most engineers of envisioning the mysterious reaches of our new quantum mechanics; while the editors of *The Bulletin of the Atomic Scientists* know that poetry is worth more than pushpin.

So far as the physical and natural sciences are concerned with general ideas and the pursuit of truth, men of humane and social studies still can be interested in the sciences and can profit from them. Even I can. But, decayed though scientific understanding may be in such quarters, the average nonscientific mind is not yet altogether unable to understand scientific vocabulary and aims—granted a little painful application. But the science must be genuine: not scientism or simple technological aggrandizement. And if "science" is converted into ideology, a substitute for philosophy and religion, then rightly men of humane and social imagination will recoil from the fraud.

In our time, the principal contributions to knowledge have been made in the physical and natural sciences; to be ignorant of science, therefore, is to neglect whatever the men of the past hundred years and more have added to human wisdom. And, as I have suggested already, a competent knowledge of science is necessary for the control of that technology which is science's progeny. These are our true reasons for serious study of science: for wisdom's sake, and for self-defense against *Brave New World* and *1984*.

Sir Charles Snow, however, and gentlemen of like mind, manifest small desire for the wisdom that one seeks through pure science; nor, doting upon modern technology, industrialism, and social change wrought through scientific discovery as positively advantageous, do they have serious misgivings about the future condition of mankind (supposing that war can be avoided). Though Snow recognizes perfunctorily some virtues in "traditional culture," his heart clearly yearns after "scientific culture": that is, after a science-oriented, technology-dominated civil social order, managed on rationalistic principles, and no nonsense. In this "scientific culture," poverty will be abolished throughout the world, over-population will have been eliminated, and there will be no danger of a nuclear war. Also, one gathers, "antisocial" and "reactionary" elements, like our most eminent men of letters in this century, will have got lost in the shuffle. Sir Charles implies that (Communist) China is well along this happy road to the joyous life of scientized society, getting over the industrial hump between the poor countries and the rich.[2]

So what Snow pursues, it turns out, is not science for the sake of science, but scientific technology for the sake of scientism. With Bacon, he looks upon science as a source of power over man and nature. His "scientific culture" is the ideology of rationalism. Despite all the penetrating criticism of scientism by real scientists and other scholars in recent years, a dogmatic confidence in the omnicompetence of science, held with all the quasi-religious zeal of Comte, lives undiminished in some members of the older scientific generation like Snow.[3] He sounds like H. G. Wells before Well's disillusion set in. Smug in this positivistic scientism of the twenties and thirties, Snow sneers at George Orwell, with his reactionary (despite his being a Socialist) attachment to "traditional culture": Orwell's *1984* is "the strongest possible wish that the future should not exist." (Incidentally, scientifically considered, the future *does* not exist—except in imagination.) It is with some justice that Snow selects Orwell for his antagonist; one has only to turn to Orwell's *Road to Wigan Pier* to find a denunciation of the "scientific culture" of the future (as lauded by a gentleman of Sir Charles' persuasion) that might have been hurled at Snow himself, had Orwell lived long enough:

. . . from that line of talk about "heaven on earth," you can make a fairly good guess at what he would like civilization to be; a sort of Lyons Corner House lasting *in saecula saeculorum* and getting bigger and noisier all the

---

[2] C. P. Snow, *The Two Cultures and the Scientific Revolution* (New York, 1959), 44. What scientific evidence does Snow provide to prove the prosperity of Communist China, in the face of the many reliable accounts of famine and industrial failure? Why, none. But the Communist Chinese are science-minded, aren't they? And they've smashed the ancient literary culture of China, haven't they? Well, then—after this fashion the *a priori* reformer always has reasoned —how could scientific planning possibly go wrong? The wish is father to the "scientific" fact.

[3] For very recent criticism of the scientistic ideology, see Wiggins and Schoeck (eds.), *Scientism and Values* (New York, 1960). Two essays by the present author touch on the subject: "Segments of Political Science Not Amenable to Behavioristic Treatment" and "Is Social Science Scientific?"

Two essays by Dr. Glenn Tinder, published in *The Review of Politics*, dissect the prevalent utilitarian view of politics: "Human Estrangement and the Failure of Political Imagination" (October, 1959), and "Modern Society and the Realms of Spirit" (January, 1961).

time. And in any book by anyone who feels at home in the machine-world —in any book by H. G. Wells, for instance—you will find passages of the same kind. How often have we not heard it, that glutinously uplifting stuff about "the machines, our new race of slaves, which will set humanity free," etc., etc., etc. To these people, apparently, the only danger of the machine is its possible use for destructive purposes; as, for instance, aeroplanes are used in war. Barring wars and unforeseen disasters, the future is envisaged as an ever more rapid march of mechanical progress; machines to save pain, hygiene, efficiency, organization, more hygiene, more efficiency, more organization, more machines—until finally you land up in the by now familiar Wellsian Utopia, aptly caricatured by Huxley in *Brave New World,* the paradise of little fat men. Of course in their daydreams of the future the little fat men are neither fat nor little; they are Men Like Gods. But why should they be? All mechanical progress is towards greater and greater efficiency; ultimately, therefore, towards a world in which *nothing goes wrong.* But in a world in which nothing went wrong, many of the qualities which Mr. Wells regards as "godlike" would be no more valuable than the animal faculty of moving the ears.

To Snow, Orwell and T. S. Eliot and Yeats and all sorts of other "traditional culture" folk are "Luddites," interfering with our wonderful machines that will serve us in the Terrestrial Paradise. Though many people think of Snow as a scientist, in fact he is a professional popular novelist—much inferior to Orwell, or to Wells, in that discipline—who long ago obtained a scientific degree at Cambridge. In the empire of science, Snow's principal achievement was administrative—recruiting scientific personnel during World War Two. His view is more nearly characteristic of the bureaucrat than of the man of truly scientific passion, intent on discovering the nature of things.

The cult of scientism ordinarily is as shoddy in its history and political theory as in its understanding of real science. Sir Charles Snow is no exception. Despite his concern with the problems of overpopulation, for instance, he confuses the relationships among child mortality, the Industrial Revolution, and the growth of cities at the expense of rural population. People want industrial life, he says, for "with singular unanimity, in any country where they have had the chance, the poor have walked off the land into the factories as fast as the factories could take them." In this cavalier fashion, he ignores the decline of infant mortality (produced by the improvement of medicine toward the end of the seventeenth century) that

caused the European population to rise abruptly in the first half of
the eighteenth century, and so made industrialization necessary for
clothing and feeding the new multitudes: the rural poor went to the
"hell holes" primarily because it was a question of becoming factory
hands or starving—not a matter of volition. I select this one oversim-
plification, among many in Snow's writings, merely to suggest that
the "scientific culture" which Snow eulogizes has no great regard for
the stubborn facts of human history or even the stubborn facts of
natural and physical science.

Despite all his concern to be contemporary—indeed, futuristic—
Sir Charles Snow is an old-fangled rationalist, almost pre-
industrialist. The system he advocates owes little enough to
twentieth-century scientific discovery, or even twentieth-century
technology; but it is thoroughly rooted in eighteenth-century rigid
rationalism. His contempt for "traditional culture" and his admiration for the material energies of Communist Russia and China are
part and parcel of this decaying ideology. Few writers illustrate
better than Snow the description of the rationalist's view of education which we have from Professor Michael Oakeshott:

From the earliest days of his emergence, the Rationalist has taken an omi-
nous interest in education. He has a respect for "brains," a great belief in
training them, and is determined that cleverness shall be encouraged and
shall receive its reward of power. But what is this education in which the
Rationalist believes? It is certainly not an initiation into the moral and intellectual habits and achievements of his society, an entry into the part-
nership between present and past, a sharing of concrete knowledge; for the
Rationalist, all this would be education in nescience, both valueless and
mischievous. It is a training in technique, a training, that is, in the half of
knowledge which can be learnt from books when they are used as cribs.
And the Rationalist's affected interest in education escapes the suspicion of
being a mere subterfuge for imposing himself more firmly on society, only
because it is clear that he is as deluded as his pupils. He sincerely believes
that a training in technical knowledge is the only education worth while,
because he is moved by the faith that there is no knowledge, in the proper
sense, except technical knowledge. He believes that a training in "public
administration" is the surest defence against the flattery of a demagogue
and the lies of a dictator. . . . The rationalist inspiration has now invaded
and has begun to corrupt the genuine educational provisions and institutions of our society: some of the ways and means by which, hitherto, a genuine (as distinct from a merely technical) knowledge has been imparted
have already disappeared, others are obsolescent, and others again are in

process of being corrupted from the inside. The whole pressure of the circumstances of our time is in this direction.

Well! If the "scientific culture" of Snow and his group means the destruction of our intellectual inheritance for the greater glory of "technique"; if "science" is understood to mean an all-embracing ideology which supplants established modes of politics and the traditions of civility; if the object of science is the realization of a future in which everyone will be just like everyone else—why, it is no wonder that men of humane studies and other nonscientific disciplines boggle at embracing the tenets of this intellectual creed. To be a know-nothing is preferable to being extinct.

I do not exaggerate Snow's advocacy of the hegemony of "scientific culture." In the moral life, he says, scientists are "the soundest group of intellectuals we have; there is a moral component right in the grain of science itself, and almost all scientists form their own judgments of the moral life." The world must be theirs—including the social scientists', of course, since they agree with Snow (at least the American ones do) in decrying literary and traditional culture. Nor must political constitutions be permitted to stand in the way of "scientific" grand designs for the betterment of the species: "People will ask me . . . 'Can you imagine a political technique, in parliamentary societies like the U.S. or our own, by which any such plan could become real?'" Why, science must fix all that. The Russians have shown the way, planning their education altogether for material production. "They have a deeper insight into the scientific revolution than we have, or than the Americans have."

If indeed Snow's scientistic rationalism were true science, then we might well feel—in Henry Adams' phrase—like monkeys monkeying with a loaded shell, suspecting that it is going to hurt us. To indoctrinate the surviving nonscientific minds in the catechism of science as the way to Brummagem Utopia would be the death of all other branches of the higher learning. And in the end, ideological scientism would give the quietus to pure science itself.

But modern science ought not to be judged by the utterances of its bureaucrats and vulgarizers. The genuine scientist of our time is not afflicted by Sir Charles Snow's *hybris;* he does not lay claim to the offices of priest, ruler, and artist. With some annoyance, even Snow remarks that many of the younger scientists, and most of the engineers, actually are conservative.

From the mechanism and materialism of much eighteenth- and nineteenth-century science, nowadays we are entering upon a natural and physical science which is something far better than the servile tool of technology. Physics is shading into metaphysics again, with Heisenberg's principle of indeterminacy; the coelacanth, that quick fossil, shakes the doctrinaire Darwinians. Exciting and mysterious, twentieth-century science truly is an integral part of liberal education, rather than a presumptuous substitute for religion, politics, and humane studies.

As it was at its dawning, in Aristotle's time, science is once more philosophical, and the wonder of Paracelsus resumes precedence over the aggrandizement of Bacon. Because it offers so much for the mind, science now attracts a disproportionate share of the more active intellects of the rising generation. Academic philosophy, for instance, at most universities and colleges, has succumbed to the death-urge of logical positivism; and professors of philosophy are reduced to keen mosquitoes who can demonstrate, to their own infinite satisfaction, the impossibility of making any satisfactory statement about anything in heaven or earth. What seeker after wisdom, this being so, would not turn to physics, rather than formal philosophy, for insight into being?

Similarly, the teaching of literature has fallen victim to primitivism and pedantry—to "communications skills," linguistics, arid philology, "creative writing," "contemporary literature," "world literature," and all the other boondoggles out of Pandora's box. In such circumstances, why wonder that the former students of humanities find astronomy or paleontology more poetic than Old Gorse?

Political science and sociology are given over to pseudo-statisticians and nose-counters; history, too often, has become the meaningless accumulation of petty detail. Clumsily imitating the natural and physical sciences, the humane and social studies have lost their old character without acquiring the high repute of real science. So science is king in the university, principally because it demands intellectual labor, and often requires high imagination.

This vigorous science is not really an enemy of the other branches of learning—not even to theology, though at the turn of the century these two seemed bitterly inimical. If one reads so good a book as Dr. William Pollard's *Chance and Providence,* one perceives how far the scientists have come since the heyday of Darwin's Bulldog.

Science and liberal learning ought not to be opposed to each other, as Snow would have them; and certainly the vestiges of literary culture ought not to be swallowed up by the technician masquerading as scientist and world reformer. Humane and social studies ought to be integrated with scientific courses, to the strengthening of both. I hasten to add that I do not advocate the pablum of even more amorphous survey courses; already "Natural Science Survey 101" is destroying the virility of college scientific disciplines; and if we do not call a halt, the purported integration (actual hybridizing and dehydrating) of knowledge will end in one gigantic fifteen-credit course called "Human Learning" or "Man."

Rather, a sound college education ought to be a strict and lively and harmonious arrangement of studies in real science and in genuinely humane subjects; and from this curriculum, the merely technical and vocational aspects of science need to be pruned, and the frivolous or pedantic aspects of "traditional culture" need to be rooted up. The same reform can be accomplished in the secondary schools. As a scholar of first-rate scientific knowledge and first-rate humane understanding—Alfred North Whitehead—pointed out, there is not room in the school day for everything that the classical curriculum included, and everything that the zealots of science would like. But the best of both fields can be preserved and strengthened, to their common benefit; and Whitehead makes some most practical suggestions.[4]

It is no paradox that the decay—almost the death—of classical studies has increased the separation between scientific and non-scientific disciplines. The Greek and Latin roots of scientific terminology, for instance, made it possible for a man of humane schooling to understand most of the vocabulary of science—while he still had Latin and Greek. Now that the "non-science" graduate is reduced to business English and the newest Webster, scientific terminology all too literally is Greek to him.

In much else, science and humane studies need each another's counsel and sympathy. The natural and physical sciences require the humanizing and poetic influences of "traditional culture," if they are to be saved from the grim utilitarian domination—the death of imagination, on which scientific advance depends—relished by Sir Charles Snow. The humane and social studies require, in this their

[4] See the essays "Mathematics and Liberal Education," and "Science in General Education," in Alfred North Whitehead, *Essays in Science and Philosophy* (New York, 1948).

hour of desiccation, the vitality and reality of scientific inquiry. Out of love of learning—which is its own end—those of us who hold by traditional culture ought to acquaint ourselves with scientific thought; and, like the scientists themselves, we must restore the just claims of pure science if we are to avert the triumph of scientism and its social consequences.

This task, after all, is not really onerous. There are men of science who write most readably: Dr. Loren Eiseley, for instance. If we take up his book *The Firmament of Time*, we find within it a powerful antidote to the dismal arrogance of Snow. Take this moving passage:

Progress secularized, progress which pursues only the next invention, progress which pulls thought out of the mind and replaces it with idle slogans, is not progress at all. It is a beckoning mirage in a desert over which stagger the generations of men. Because man, each individual man among us, possesses his own soul and by that light must live or perish, there is no way by which Utopias—or the lost Garden itself—can be brought out of the future and presented to man. Neither can he go forward to such a destiny. Since in the world of time every man lives but one life, it is in himself that he must search for the secret of the Garden. With the fading of religious emphasis and the growth of the torrent, modern man is confused. The tumult without has obscured those voices that still cry desperately to man from somewhere within his consciousness.[5]

In the manifesto of Sir Charles Snow, one hears only the tumult of the torrent: the flood waters are out, and we are borne down to the Dead Sea. But in the words of a scholar of science who knows that intuition and tradition are quite as scientific as Univac, we perceive that systematic learning which is the natural partner of the sacred and the humane.

[5] Loren Eiseley, *The Firmament of Time* (New York, 1960), 140.

RELIGION, MORALS, AND CULTURE

The Rarity of
the God-Fearing Man

A Michigan farmer, some years ago, climbed to the roof of his silo, and there he painted, in great red letters that the Deity could see, "The fear of the Lord is the beginning of wisdom." These words are on that roof yet. When in his cups, which was often enough, that farmer thrashed his daughter to fill her with a holy terror.

In his way, I suppose, the drunken brute did fear God. Surviving the thrashings, his daughter grew to be a woman; and though she did not much fancy her father's company, she lived as decent a life as most. Her upbringing, bad though it was, may have been better than the formative years of the average American child nowadays, "permissively" reared. To the permitted brat with the permissive parents, few appetites are denied, and he grows up ignorant of the norms of human existence. Never learning in childhood that certain things exist which we ought to fear, he slides into physical maturity, bored, flabby in character, and moved by irrational impulses toward violence and defiance, the consequence of a profound disorder in personality.

Without a knowledge of fear, we cannot know order in personality or society. Fear forms an ineluctable part of the human condition. Fear lacking, hope and aspiration fail. To demand for mankind "freedom from fear," as politically attainable, was a silly piece of demagogic sophistry. If, *per impossibile,* fear were wiped altogether out of our lives, we would be desperately bored, yearning for old or new terrors; vegetating, we would cease to be human beings. A child's fearful joy in stories of goblins, witches, and ghosts is a natural yearning after the challenge of the dreadful: raw head and bloody bones, in one form or another, the imagination demands. From the great instinct to survive, to struggle, to triumph, comes the urge to contend with fear.

And there are things which rightfully we ought to fear, if we are to enjoy any dignity as men. When, in an age of smugness and softness, fear has been pushed temporarily into the dark corners of personality and society, then soon the gods of the copybook headings with fire and sword return. To fear to commit evil, and to hate what is abominable, is the mark of manliness. "They will never love where they ought to love," Burke says, "who do not hate where they ought to hate." It may be added that they will never dare when they ought to dare, who do not fear when they ought to fear.

Time was when there lay too heavy upon man that fear of the Lord which is the beginning of wisdom. Soul-searching can sink into morbidity, and truly conscience can make cowards of us all. Scotland in the seventeenth century, for instance, tormented itself into a kind of spiritual hypochondria by an incessant melancholy fawning upon the Lord's favor. But no such age is ours.

Forgetting that there exists such a state as salutary dread, modern man has become spiritually foolhardy. His bravado, I suspect, will stand the test no better than ancient Pistol's. He who admits no fear of God is really a post-Christian man; for at the heart of Judaism and Christianity lies a holy dread. And a good many people, outwardly and perhaps inwardly religious—for *religio* implies the cult, the common worship, the binding together, rather than the relationship between the Almighty and lonely man—today deny the reality of reverential fear, and thus are post-Christian without confessing it.

Christianity always was a scandal; and I rather think I began to fear God because I discovered that terror to be so unconventional, impractical, and off-color in our era. (Men are moved in divers ways, and belief actually will follow action.) Before I began to think much on the spiritual diseases of our century, I revolted against the disgusting smugness of modern America—particularly the complacency of professors and clergymen, the flabby clerisy of a sensate time. Once I found myself in a circle of scholars who were discussing solemnly the conditions necessary for arriving at scientific truth. Chiefly from a perverse impulse to shock this Academy of Lagado, perhaps, I muttered, "We have to begin with the dogma that the fear of God is the beginning of wisdom."

I succeeded in scandalizing. Some gentlemen and scholars took this for indecent levity; others, unable to convince themselves that anyone could mean this literally, groped for the presumptive allegorical or symbolical meaning behind my words. But two or three churchgoers in the gathering were not displeased. These were given to passing the collection plate and to looking upon the church as a means to social reform; incense, vestments, and the liturgy have their aesthetic charms, even among doctors of philosophy. Faintly pleased, yes, these latter professors, to hear the echo of fife and drum ecclesiastic; but also embarrassed at such radicalism. "Oh no," they murmured, "not the *fear* of God. You mean the *love* of God, don't you?"

For them the word of Scripture was no warrant, their Anglo-Catholicism notwithstanding. With Henry Ward Beecher, they were eager to declare that God is Love—though hardly a love which passes all understanding. Theirs was a thoroughly permissive God the Father, properly instructed by Freud. Looking upon their mild and diffident faces, I wondered how much trust I might put in such love as they knew. Their meekness was not that of Moses. Meek before Jehovah, Moses had no fear of Pharoah; but these doctors of the schools, much at ease in Zion, were timid in the presence of a traffic policeman. Although convinced that God is too indulgent to punish much of anything, they were given to trembling before Caesar. Christian love is the willingness to sacrifice oneself; yet I

would not have counted upon these gentlemen to adventure anything of consequence for my sake, nor even for those with greater
claims upon them. I doubted whether the Lord would adventure
much on their behalf: the vessels for dishonor are not necessarily the
sots of Skid Row. If, for instance, there should come a moment in
which these particular churchgoers should be confronted with the
squalid oligarchs of our time, the gauleiters and the commissars
—why, I would look for precious little sacrifice from them.
Theirs was a light love. Gauleiters and commissars? Why, their
fellowship and charity were not proof against a dean or a
divisional head.

"Me supreme Wisdom and primal Love sustain": this is the legend
above the gate of the Inferno. The great grim Love which makes
Hell a part of the nature of things, my colleagues could not
apprehend. And, lacking knowledge of that Love, at once compas-
sionate and retributive, their sort may bring us presently to a
terrestrial hell, which is the absence of God from the affairs of
men—with certain unattractive personal and social consequences.

In ceasing to fear God, their sort would find themselves, soon or
late, naked before earthly frights; in mistaking God for a Sunday-
afternoon dad reading the comics, or for a progressive kindergarten
teacher, they would dawdle down the path to the bushes at the
bottom of the garden—and find behind the prickly pear the King of
Terrors. The guillotine made a Christian of the mocking La Harpe;
the humanitarian professor made a God-fearing man of me.

Religiosity, or at least a festive and indolent and church-plate-
passing Sabbatarianism, is sufficiently established in our America.
But the God-fearing man is sufficiently rare among us, and not
noticeably welcome in pulpit or pew. I have known of ministers
given the sack by their congregations for fretting overmuch about the
wrath of the Lord; indeed, there is ample precedent for this,
Jonathan Edwards, our only theologian of mark, having been
pushed into the backwoods for precisely such excess of zeal. Not
many among us subscribe to James Fitzjames Stephen's concept of
God, though it is orthodox enough:

I think of [this Being] as conscious and having will, as infinitely powerful,
and as one who, whatever he may be in his own nature, has so arranged
the world or worlds in which I live as to let me know that virtue is the law
which he has prescribed to me and to others. If still further asked, Can you

love such a Being? I should answer, Love is not the word which I should choose, but awe. The law under which we live is stern, and, as far as we can judge, inflexible, but it is noble and excites a feeling of awful respect for its Author and for the constitution established in the world which it governs, and a sincere wish to act up to and carry it out as far as possible. If we believe in God at all, this, I think, is the rational and manly way of thinking of him.[1]

With Stephen's description of God as judge, it is not unprofitable to contrast the vision of the Lord vouchsafed to a certain immensely rich and well-known living American, eminently successful in business and politics. This gentleman freely confesses that he is not wholly a self-made man: God loves him and has helped him on his way. "God always has his arm around my shoulder." As a species of junior partner, God has been properly permissive and submissive. Our successful American does not fear God. Why in Heaven's name should he? God knows his place.

Every age portrays God in the image of its poetry and its politics. In one century, God is an absolute monarch, exacting his due; in another century, still an absolute sovereign, but a benevolent despot; again, perhaps a grand gentleman among aristocrats; at a different time, a democratic president, with an eye to the ballot box. It has been said that to many of our generation, God is a Republican and works in a bank; but this image is giving way, I think, to God as Chum—at worst, God as a playground supervisor. So much for the images. But in reality God does not alter.

Because the graven image deludes, it is forbidden. Yet a mental image of some sort men demand, in any time. C. S. Lewis tells of a small girl who, on inquiring of her parents what God looked like, was carefully informed that God is a Perfect Substance. To the girl, a Perfect Substance meant tapioca pudding; and since she detested tapioca pudding, she grew up with a marked prejudice against God. God the patriarch, with the flowing white beard, is perhaps as true an image as little girls or big ones are likely to hit upon. The deceptive image, formed by our petty preferences in taste or politics, may do remarkable mischief. And God the Chum, never to be dreaded because He is indiscriminately affectionate—even promiscuous —may be a more treacherous idol, and more potent for the

[1] James Fitzjames Stephen, *Liberty, Equality, Fraternity* (London, 1873), 45–46.

destruction of personality and of the civil social order, than the vision of God that had Agag hewed in pieces.

If in Scripture one thing is beyond dispute, it is the injunction to fear God. But in this enlightened era it is almost blasphemous to whisper this awkward doctrine in the sensitive ears of churchgoing folk. A vulgarized Pelagianism proscribes the description of sinners in the hands of an angry God; and, correspondingly, the idea of a retributive Providence is out of fashion. So far as Providence really is credited at all by most professed Christians in 1965, that Providence is regularly beneficent, dispensing fur coats and Jaguars. Hints to the contrary are more often encountered in the writings of philosophical historians than in sermons. It must come as a shock to many positivistic professors of history to read Professor Herbert Butterfield's account of the workings of Providence; for Butterfield's is the archaic, orthodox, calm, and ultimately hopeful view that Providence is the operation of laws made for man, immutable and at least as often destructive as rewarding. "If atomic research should by some accident splinter and destroy this whole globe tomorrow," Mr. Butterfield writes in his *Christianity in History,*

I imagine that it will hurt us no more than that 'death on the road' under the menace of which we pass every day of our lives. It will only put an end to a globe which we always knew was doomed to a bad end in any case. I am not sure that it would not be typical of human history if—assuming that the world was bound some day to cease to be a possible habitation for living creatures—men should by their own contrivance hasten that end and anticipate the operation of nature or of time—because it is so much in the character of Divine judgment in history that men are made to execute it upon themselves.[2]

Yes, this has become unpopular doctrine. Despite the catastrophes of our century, despite the evidence of the newspapers that the fountains of the great deep are broken up, the meliorism of the Enlightenment—now what the sociologists call a cultural lag, but none the less pervasive for that—still dominates all classes of modern society. In some quarters, it has assumed the ideological form of apocalyptic Marxism; in others, the garments of a "progressive people's capitalism," with its "revolution of rising expectations"; or it may be blended with the "Freudian ethic," managing somehow

[2] Herbert Butterfield, *Christianity in History* (London, 1950), 66.

to reconcile with the womb-gloom of Freud a cheerful confidence that all will be well if only we soothe and adjust and recognize or liberate repressed desires—and pay the psychiatrist. This obsolete but persistent meliorism inspires the rosy dreams of a universal political system, to be attained almost instanter by the United Nations Organization or some other instrument, despite the clearly centrifugal motion of twentieth-century nationalism.

Probably the most influential popularizer of these notions was John Stuart Mill, with his conviction that if only want, disease, and war should be abolished—through economic progress and positive law—the human condition would be hunky-dory. Mill, rather than St. Augustine, is the authority for post-Christian man; and Stephen's concept of God was inconceivable to Mill. How can we fear what rationalism cannot demonstrate?

"Do you feel happy inside?" asks the modern young minister in Marquand's *Women and Thomas Harrow*. That clergyman himself is trapped into confessing that he often does not feel happy inside; but it never would do to let slip such heresies from the pulpit. What renewed consciousness of the need for fearing the Lord as has been expressed in our century, often has come from quarters notoriously unclerical. We find, for instance, a striking passage in Bernard Shaw's preface to *Back to Methuselah:* "Goodnatured unambitious men," Shaw observes, "are cowards when they have no religion." Before the spectacle of half of Europe being kicked to death by the other half, they stare in helpless horror, or are persuaded by the newspapers that this is a sound commercial investment and an act of divine justice:

They are dominated and exploited not only by greedy and often half-witted and half-alive weaklings who will do anything for cigars, champagne, motor cars, and the more childish and selfish uses of money, but by able and sound administrators who can do nothing else with them than dominate and exploit them. Government and exploitation become synonymous under such circumstances; and the world is finally ruled by the childish, the brigands, and the blackguards.

Such is the post-Christian man, contemptuous of God but fearful of everything else, for whom Shaw would have invented a new sort of faith. Politically, the man who does not fear God is prey to the squalid oligarchs; and this is no paradox. What raises up heroes and martyrs is the fear of God. Beside the terror of God's judgment, the atrocities of the totalist tyrant are pinpricks. A God-intoxicated man, knowing that divine love and divine wrath are but different aspects of a unity, is sustained against the worst this world can do to him; while the goodnatured unambitious man, lacking religion, fearing no ultimate judgment, denying that he is made for eternity, has in him no iron to maintain order and justice and freedom.

Mere enlightened self-interest will submit to any strong evil. In one aspect or another, fear insists upon forcing itself into our lives. If the fear of God is obscured, then obsessive fear of suffering, poverty, and sickness will come to the front; or if a well-cushioned state keeps most of these worries at bay, then the tormenting neuroses of modern man, under the labels of "insecurity" and "anxiety" and "constitutional inferiority," will be the dominant mode of fear. And these latter forms of fear are the more dismaying, for there are disciplines by which one may diminish one's fear of God. But to remedy the causes of fear from the troubles of our time is beyond the power of the ordinary individual; and to put the neuroses to sleep, supposing any belief in a transcendent order to be absent, there is only the chilly comfort of the analyst's couch or the tranquillizing drug.

By the fashionable philodoxies of our modern era, by our dominant system of education, by the tone of the serious and the popular press, by the assumptions of the politicians, by most of the sermons to the churchgoers, post-Christian man has been persuaded to do what man always has longed to do—that is, to forget the fear of the Lord. And with that fear have also departed his wisdom and his courage. Only a ferocious drunken farmer is unenlightened enough to affirm a primary tenet of religion in great red letters, and he does not know its meaning. Freedom from fear, if I read St. John aright, is one of the planks in the platform of the Antichrist. But that freedom is delusory and evanescent, and is purchased only at the cost of spiritual and political enslavement. It ends at Armageddon. So in our time, as Yeats saw,

> Things fall apart; the centre cannot hold;
> Mere anarchy is loosed upon the world,
> The blood-dimmed tide is loosed, and everywhere
> The ceremony of innocence is drowned;
> The best lack all conviction, while the worst
> Are full of passionate intensity.

Lacking conviction that the fear of the Lord is the beginning of wisdom, the captains and the kings yield to the fierce ideologues, the merciless adventurers, the charlatans and the metaphysically mad. And then, truly, when the stern and righteous God of fear and love has been denied, the Savage God lays down his new commandments.

Sincere God-fearing men, I believe, are now a scattered remnant. Yet as it was with Isaiah, so it may yet be with us, that disaster brings consciousness of that stubborn remnant and brings, too, a renewed knowledge of the source of wisdom. Truth and hardihood may find a lodging in some modern hearts when the new schoolmen and the parsons, or some of them, are brought to confess that it is a terrible thing to be delivered into the hands of the living God.

In a Michigan college town stands an immense quasi-Gothic church building, and the sign upon the porch informs the world that this is "The People's Church, Nondenominational and Nonsectarian." Sometimes, passing by, a friend of mine murmurs, "The People's Church—formerly God's." In The People's Church, the sermons have to do with the frightful evils of beer and cigarettes; all too probably, such townsfolk as are not present on the Sabbath have sunk themselves in these sins; and the congregation is congratulated by their pastor on their godliness in occupying the pews. A heavy complacency glows faintly in the eyes of these good people.

From The People's Church, the fear of God, with its allied wisdom, has been swept away. So have I. Who could fear a teetotaling, nonsmoking, nondenominational, nonsectarian God? Not the professors and the shopkeepers and the landladies of this happy college town. If by any amazing chance they ever should find themselves in God's hands—which is beyond reason, since they know that the real purpose of the church is merely to serve as a moral police—the members of this virtuous congregation, surely, would simply be patted and soothed like spaniels.

From this post-Christian church the fear of God, together with the odor of sanctity, has been cleansed quite away. In the cleansing, the college has assisted. Within the doors there remains, spiritually considered, only a vacuum—which nature abhors. Presently something will fill that vacuum; and it may be a rough beast, its hour come round at last, with the stench of death in its fur.

The Impenitent Religionist:
American Protestantism Today

*I*n every suburb of the United States, new churches rise, most of them in the modern manner: simple of line, sparing of decoration. Their architects, for the most part, have broken with American and European traditions. Their lines are the work of twentieth-century taste and technology. These churches have never been more prosperous. Institutional Christianity seems triumphant, and the majority of American Christians remain Protestant—some sixty-three million of them, from High-Church Episcopalians to Jehovah's Witnesses.

Yet some American Protestants are disquieted. The architecture of suburban churches has been adapted to the temper of the twentieth century. Can the spirit and influence of Protestant Christianity, however, prevail in a suburbanized, industrialized, standardized, centralized, immensely prosperous modern America? Is traditional Protestantism, despite its outward success, beginning to lose its power over consciences and the tone of society? Some of the shrewdest friendly critics of Protestantism think so.

The late Albert Jay Nock once said that every nation has an established church, whether or not it admits the fact; and the establishd church of the United States—according to Nock, who was once an Episcopal minister—was the Methodist and Baptist lobby in Washington. If the statement ever had any validity, it is obvious that it doesn't have much now. American Protestantism is greatly changing, and perhaps losing much influence; Dr. Martin Marty, associate editor of the weekly *Christian Century,* has been prompted to assert that America is in a post-Protestant era.

Endeavoring to analyze the changing climate of religious opinion, I traveled for two months, from New England to California, and from Montana to Florida. I talked with nearly two hundred Protestant clergy and laymen, and with a good many Catholics and Jews. I corresponded with a hundred more. Over the past several years I have addressed various groups of ministers and have lectured occasionally at seminaries; I have read the principal Christian magazines attentively and most of the numerous recent books that discuss religion in America. During annual trips abroad over the past decade, I have examined Christian opinions and Christian churches in western Europe, comparing these with American tendencies. What follows, then, is a summary of the principal problems and prospects for Protestantism in the United States. I have found grave difficulties, but also signs of real vitality.

About 35 percent of all Americans belong to Protestant churches. (By way of contrast, when the United States began only some 5 percent of the people claimed church membership; in 1850, only about 12 percent.) Protestants still outnumber Catholics, of whom there are some forty-one million, or about 24 percent of the population. (For a century, Catholics have been slowly gaining on Protestants in church membership, but there seems to be small probability that they will outnumber Protestants in the predictable future.) This church membership percentage figure perhaps represents the saturation point in a country where there is no legal compulsion to attend services and where dread of hellfire is rare.

In comparison with Protestantism in England and Scandinavia, American Protestantism has a wide popular appeal. In Denmark, for instance, less than one half of one percent of the population retains any active church connection. Dogmatic atheism is nearly extinct in the United States, and there has flourished since World War Two an American Protestant revival on several levels of belief and method.

Also American Protestantism is a very big business. In recent years, gifts to its churches have exceeded three billion dollars annually. An interesting point here is that contributions are highest per capita among the Fundamentalist groups: e.g., Free Methodist, Seventh-day Adventist, Church of the Nazarene, Southern Baptist. Approximately one billion dollars will be spent for church construction this year. Even in decayed city centers, almost no churches are derelict. Many city churches are heavily endowed. The principal denominations operate their own life insurance and annuity systems; one—the Aid Association for Lutherans in Wisconsin—has nearly one and a half billion dollars in policies in force.

The Protestant denominations still control, support, or retain some connection with over five hundred colleges and universities. (This, however, represents a decline, in several denominations, from the number of colleges once maintained.) And some three hundred and forty thousand pupils are enrolled in Protestant church-related elementary and secondary schools. Such famous seminaries as Union, General, Harvard, Yale, Princeton, and Virginia Theological are magnificently endowed, and ample funds are available for the support of any promising divinity student. Protestant church presses publish hundreds of books annually, and they make money; the total monthly circulation of Protestant church magazines is more than fifteen million. The compensation of ministers, improving in recent years, now averages something better than six thousand dollars a year in the major denominations. Like America generally, the Protestant churches have boomed in this century; they fit snugly—perhaps too comfortably—into the fabric of American society.

But the criticism is that the heart of Protestantism is not so sound as the rosy flush of worldly success might suggest. One of the most knowing critics of religion in America is the theologian Dr. Will Herberg of Drew University. Protestantism—and for that matter, Catholicism and Judaism—he feels, does not deeply affect the lives of Americans. The United States has embraced a religion-in-general that is "progressively evacuated of content."[1] Christianity remains socially approved; but it amounts to little more than a vague spirit of friendliness, a willingness to support churches—provided these churches demand no real sacrifices and preach no exacting doctrines. This climate of opinion Herberg calls "the ethos of sociability"; and it is a far cry from the demands and the intensely personal and searching character of earlier Protestantism.

Pessimism about the actual influence of Protestant doctrine is not confined to theologians and sociologists. A minister in a small Wisconsin town says, "People seem to have stopped reading the Bible, stopped thinking about theology, sometimes, it seems, almost stopped thinking. They just go through the motions."

Richard Rice, an editor of Methodist Sunday school publications, makes a similar indictment: "Protestantism, at the grass-roots level, has degenerated into sentimentality, partly as a result of democracy and partly as a result of prosperity," he told me. "Say we Americans: 'Everything ought to be useful, even religion; now, really, why shouldn't we be happy and cheerful in church? And, you meet the nicest people in church.' What is so discouraging about this religiosity," said Rice, "is that, for a while at least, it works. People in droves come to church."

But meanwhile, despite all the churchgoing, there is the widespread increase in immorality. For centuries, ardent Protestants expected church membership to be reflected in an improved private and public morality, an elevation of mind and character, and a

---

[1] Among American Jews, the decline of doctrinal convictions seems to have gone even further than among Protestants; many Jews give as their principal reason for attending the synagogue the argument that "it holds the family together." Among American Catholics, the visible decay of active belief is checked somewhat by the authoritative hierarchical and doctrinal system of the Catholic church; yet most American Catholics, too, seem to be deeply influenced by "the ethos of sociability," and the Vatican has long feared what is called "Americanism" among Catholics in this country—that is, the gradual absorption of Catholic laymen and even clergy into an American "religion-in-general." But, being conscious minorities, Catholics and Jews are more aware of the danger to themselves of being drawn altogether into secular humanitarianism and a beaming complacency.

better society. But today, American Protestantism is confronted with disturbing evidence that it does not harvest the promised fruits of churchgoing. The rate of divorce moves steadily upward; so does the rate of crime. Drugstore racks are crowded with salacious magazines and paperbacks; the services of the psychiatrist are more and more in demand; sexual perversion and addiction to narcotics flourish in a bored age. Though Protestantism certainly has not brought about these phenomena, it seems clear that such gross diversions and social ills have kept pace with the growth of church attendance—almost as if the shallow religiosity and spiritual decadence were warp and woof of a cultural pattern.

If Protestantism has a center in America, it is Nashville, with some two hundred and fifty churches—nearly all of them Protestant, and most of them evangelical Protestant. (Rome, with twelve times Nashville's population of 170,870, has less than twice as many churches.) The capital of Tennessee is a center of administration and publishing for several big denominations—Church of Christ, Methodist, Southern Baptist, Seventh-day Adventist. Practically everyone goes to church on Sunday morning. Yet, Nashville's crime rate ranks seventh among American cities. Nashville's public welfare rolls are high. "Formerly we used to take care of our own, when they were in want," a Nashville Church of Christ minister said. "Now we let the state and county and city provide for them—mass charity, impersonal charity. Churches are full, yes; but they're less concerned with the duties of Christians."

Dr. Samuel Miller, dean of Harvard Divinity School, thinks that this superficial conformity to Protestant opinion cannot exist permanently side by side with an actual lack of performance. "We may see many empty churches," he told me, "in our own time." The restlessness of modern man, he says, is the product of a spiritual emptiness; and it can be remedied only by genuine restoration of the higher religious understanding, of transcendent truth, of the sense of the numinous.

The general drift of American culture is not toward a vital Protestantism. In the public schools, instruction is pretty thoroughly secularized—partly in obedience to Supreme Court decisions of the past decade—so that cursory treatment of Christian claims in the average highschool course in world history, say, must disturb the more intelligent young person who attends church or Sunday school. A Michigan farmer told me his measure of sound education: "My test of a school is this—does it teach a boy to read the Bible and explain passages of Scripture?" His was the old Protestant concept of schooling, intended to develop conscience and stimulate private judgment. The "progressive" and "permissive" doctrines that have been in vogue in the public schools for the past generation are at loggerheads with such an ideal.

In the average American parish, the primary religious discipline—the ordering of souls—has fallen into some neglect. Such a "Protestantism" without doctrines or real duties may exist for a long time, as Will Herberg remarks—supposing it encounters no stern challenges. But the passionate aspirations of Luther and Calvin and Knox and Wesley are forgotten by the cheerful conformist to the ethos of sociability. And in the twentieth century, Protestantism, like the other divisions of Christianity, is challenged by aggressive rival beliefs, of which communism is chief. Against this threat, Protestantism's trumpet has given forth an uncertain sound.

Intelligent Catholic critics are as distressed at the prospect of a declining Protestant conviction as are many leading Protestants. Father Thurston Davis, editor of the Jesuit weekly *America*, says that American Catholicism is not prepared to assume the duty of furnishing religious and moral guidance to the whole nation, on short notice; and if the Protestant churches cease to influence the mass of Americans, the alternative may be a sub-paganism. "Today," he remarks, "we are certainly not a Catholic country, or are we on the way to becoming one. But we have virtually ceased to be Protestant."

Two chief doctrines, which the Protestant reformers claimed were derived from the faith and custom of the early Christian church, distinguished the Protestant churches from others. The first of these doctrines is the necessity for a profound personal experience of salvation, through the grace of God: justification by faith. The second doctrine is what Luther called "the priesthood of all believers," the duty of every Christian to serve as priest to his fellow Christians.

Along with these convictions went a belief in the final authority of the Bible, to which every Christian might have direct recourse, as the inspired word of God; and there was an insistence upon the right and duty of private judgment within the church in theological matters, in the light of scriptural study. Out of these doctrines and practices grew the "Protestant ethic" with its emphasis upon private judgment in all things, self-reliance—a kind of democracy in religion—its advocacy of strict self-examination and self-discipline, its commendation of work, its appeal to conscience. In its beginnings, Protestantism was an austere and demanding way of life, as well as a search for personal communion with divine love and wisdom. To the old America, rural and individualistic, Protestantism was particularly suited.

But the American civilization with which Protestantism must be concerned today is not predominantly rural and is far less individualistic than it once was. Can the Protestant churches permanently win the city and the suburb? Can they appeal to the man in the factory as they appealed to the man behind the plough? Is Protestantism socially obsolete? Such questions have been raised by Protestant thinkers with growing urgency for the past thirty years and more. American Protestantism has to give more than a dusty answer.

A quarter of a century ago, Paul Tillich (anticipating Dr. Martin Marty) suggested that the Protestant era of our civilization was drawing to a close. Tillich then was influenced strongly by Marxist social theory, and he believed a tendency toward mass collectivism to be inevitable. Capitalism was in a state of advanced decay, he assumed, and social disintegration imminent; the masses would become increasingly impoverished and discontent. Since men "work in masses in big factories," he wrote, "since they, as masses, receive the same low wage; since they live as masses in the same type of run-down houses and poor streets; since, as masses, they have the same slight chances of material or intellectual enjoyment, a mass attitude tends more and more to replace more individuated ones, to subject them to the laws of mass feeling and mass emotion, and to lay them open to the appeals of every agitator who is able to use and abuse the laws of modern mass psychology." [2] Thus the frame of society and climate of opinion that nurtured the Protestant principle would go to the wall.

Now it is true that mass society has grown in power since Tillich wrote; but it is not the sort of mass society he had in mind. His predictions of impoverished working masses, at least in the United States and western Europe, seem almost comical today. The material well-being and variety of opportunity in life have increased substan-

[2] Paul Tillich, *The Protestant Era*, trans. James Luther Adams (Chicago, 1957), 223.

tially for most people. The problem for American Protestantism is not the impoverished mass-man, but the prosperous mass-man. Though the difficulties of city churches are grave, what with shifting populations, and though the shrinking of rural population troubles country clergymen—still, many ministers tell me that the hardest row for an earnest Protestant pastor to hoe is the green and cheerful suburb.

So the problems of the mass age are not the problems of poverty; the material conditions of existence steadily grow easier. Some of the causes of the decline in Protestant vigor may be suggested briefly.

First, Protestantism arose in an age of increasing individualism; it had close ties with the commercial and industrial revolutions, from the sixteenth through the nineteenth centuries, and with the rising middle classes. Private judgment in matters of religious conviction was paralleled by private judgment in economic life and in politics. But the exercise of secular private judgment is diminishing in the twentieth century. As small-scale business and local government give way to the great corporation and the centralized state, fewer and fewer people really make decisions by which they, personally, must stand or fall. And people who come to feel that they need make few important private decisions in business or politics tend to feel that they need make few important private decisions in religion or morality. Thus the Protestant principles of self-reliance and self-examination tend to atrophy.

Second, the conditions of modern industrial civilization do not strongly encourage the search after God. To the average Western man today, the good things of life appear to come almost automatically, out of factories and department stores; they seem to be man's creations and his birthright. The old-fashioned farmer knew he was dependent on God's providence; twentieth-century urban man looks to the government, the corporation, and the giant union for protection and plenty. The Protestant of yesteryear passionately sought the salvation of his soul, endeavoring to establish a personal relationship with divine mercy. The average American, some Protestants told me, now tends to tolerate God, rather than to fear Him. As one young coed remarked, "Yes, I believe in God, but I'm not nuts about Him."

Third, probably most modern men, Americans included, feel vaguely that religion, not being "scientific," need not be accepted earnestly as a guide to living. Americans still think that religion is a

Good Thing—for the children, and for uplift on Sunday morning. But their old confidence in Protestant—or Catholic, or Jewish—doctrine as the source of wisdom and worldly conduct has diminished. They may pay more attention to the new priesthood of science—though perhaps they understand scientific theory no better than they do theology. It probably is true, as Tillich writes, that "the conflict between the natural sciences and religion has been overcome in all important philosophies." It certainly is true that the physical sciences—particularly quantum physics, with Heisenberg's principle of indeterminacy—now have reentered the realm of mystery, and may be willing enough to admit the validity of metaphysics, or even of theology. Yet my wanderings in pursuit of Protestantism lead me to suspect that the typical Protestant clergyman, let alone the typical layman, is not on easy terms with "all important philosophies" of the twentieth century. Among most nominal Protestants there persists a tendency to contain scientific truth and religious affiliation in separate compartments, and sometimes to wall off from each other ethical doctrine and everyday conduct.

These are but a few of the conflicts between modern civilization and Protestant tradition. Theologians have a term, Pelagianism, to describe the malady that afflicts American Protestant churches nowadays. Pelagius was an eminent heretic of the fifth century who taught that there is no original sin; that every soul is guiltless; that man's will is wholly free; that the Grace of God is not necessary for salvation; and that, consequently, man's lot presents no serious problem of redemption.

In private life, the American Pelagian thinks, happiness may be assured by friendliness, adjustment to the community, and material improvement. In national and international affairs, all will go well if only men reason together and reconcile their interests, in a spirit of good will: thus the enthusiasm for summit conferences or their equivalent. That a lust for domination may be rooted in human nature is a doctrine rarely heard from pulpits because it goes against the grain of the average American church attender.

From complacency and Pelagianism, however, a good number of perturbed Protestant clergymen and laymen are trying to redeem the Protestant churches of America. There are heartening signs that Protestant belief and practice may confront the difficulties of the twentieth century with courage and intelligence. There are, indeed, four movements within American Protestantism that can be called such signs: the ecumenical endeavor, the theological revival, the evangelical revival, and the application of Christian ethics to modern society.

Protestantism has always been plagued by schism; and only in recent years have American Protestant churches worked with some success toward reunion. Among a little more than half of all denominations, the National Council of Churches provides a loose connection. American Protestantism's backbone is formed by the Baptists, Methodists, Lutherans, Episcopalians, and Presbyterians, with each of them divided into sects or factions. (The second largest of all Protestant denominations in the United States, the Southern Baptist, declines to belong formally to the National Council; some prefer, for historical reasons, not to be formally called Protestant. One of the historically most influential, though now comparatively small, denominations, the Unitarian, is not accepted as Christian by the National Council.) Protestantism is still further split by the existence of separate churches for white and Negro worshippers within many denominations. To establish some sort of harmony among the two hundred and thirty-odd Protestant groups, the leaders of the ecumenical movement have been earnestly at work.

Some degree of union has been attained. The Methodists have reunited, except for the Free Methodist congregations. The Lutherans effected one consolidation in 1960, and another in 1962. Only two principal divisions of Presbyterianism remain. Recently the Congregational Christian Churches and the Evangelical and Reformed Church (both the result of interdenominational mergers) merged in turn to form the United Church of Christ.

But these reunions, except for the United Church, have been *within* major denominations, rather than mergers of historically distinct churches. In December, 1960, Dr. Eugene Carson Blake and other church leaders proposed a more sweeping ecumenical project: that there should be an effective union of the Episcopal Church, the Methodist Church, the Presbyterian Church, and the United Church of Christ. The advocates of this proposal estimated that at least ten years must elapse before its consummation.

The actual interval of time will probably be longer than that, if ever such a merger comes to pass. "The National Council of Churches," said the forthright president of one evangelical seminary that I visited, "is a club for church secretaries; it doesn't reach the grass roots of Protestantism, and it doesn't much influence the theologians, or even the ministers." Differences of doctrine and church government among the members of this projected union remain great; and reunion without common belief, harmony at the expense of real doctrine, would be a Pyrrhic victory, the numerous opponents of abrupt reunion argue.

Nor does it seem probable that white and colored congregations will merge, except in some northern cities where colored Protestants have moved into downtown areas that contain churches still beloved by their dwindling white congregations. A century of separation has created strong and coherent colored denominational branches and congregations, most of them Baptist or Methodist. Integration of churches would mean diminished influence (now very strong among their laity), and diminished opportunities for advancement, for most colored ministers. The "kneel-in" demonstrations at some southern churches seem to have been more an assertion of right than an actual plea for regular merger with white congregations.

Rather than racial integration within Protestant churches, we probably will see improvement of the education of colored clergymen, and more amicable association at the ministerial level. For the past decade, all Southern Baptist seminaries have admitted Negro students freely. The Methodists also have taken steps toward more equal treatment. For that matter, the Protestants never have neglected colored members; there are thousands of Negro ministers, but very few colored Catholic priests.

In general, the people with whom I have talked seem to feel that though there obviously are real advantages in creedal agreement and efficiency of work which ought to flow from ecumenical success, still there remains the danger that churches might unite at the expense of doctrine and sincerity of belief. To discard traditional faith for the sake of a rather fuzzy good will is a perilous tendency in American Protestantism today. Besides, the major denominations have so elaborate an apparatus of church organization that many leaders remain unwilling to yield up their distinct character for the sake of a unity which might be, after all, only nominal. Although it appears that divisions will be further reduced during the next ten or twenty years, still the Episcopalians are unlikely to come to terms with the Church of God, or the Lutherans of the Missouri Synod with the Universalists. Really enduring ecumenical success must wait upon doctrinal agreement. And toward such doctrinal agreement the seminaries are making progress.

An intellectual movement, now possibly at its height, is bringing strength to the ecumenical endeavor and may succeed in waking many Protestants to the real meaning of the Christian life.

Most of the influential seminaries are substantially interdenominational nowadays, and many leading theologians, in their books and lectures, no longer identify themselves as Methodists or Presbyterians or Baptists. This is intellectual reunion, the consequence of the recovery of serious theological studies. Today it is not uncommon for Protestant divinity students to select their denomination *after* they have been graduated.

There is occurring, in short, a recovery of Protestantism from the intellectual shock which it suffered late in the nineteenth century. For eighty years or more, Christianity in general and Protestantism in particular have been battered and sometimes thrashed by the rival claims of the physical and biological sciences and by the aggressive secularism that sprang from nineteenth-century positivism, Darwinianism, and related movements. Under the assault, Protestantism split into two main camps: the Fundamentalists, always a numerical majority among American Protestants, who chose to ignore the new science and the new criticism, falling back upon simple faith and literal interpretation of the Bible; and the Liberals, who came to believe that much of the Old Testament must be discarded as barbarism, and some of the New Testament received only with caution, and optimistically embraced the nineteenth-century secular gospel of Progress.

The present theological revival may be able to rescue both Liberals and Fundamentalists from their positions. At most of the famous seminaries, there is now dominant a revived Christian orthodoxy which has strengthened itself by a strict criticism of sources and sometimes by insights drawn from the physical and natural sciences, and even from modern psychology. This theological revival is a thoroughgoing rejection of latter-day Pelagianism. The renascent orthodoxy of Protestantism returns for wisdom to St. Paul, St. Augustine, Luther, and Calvin. It perceives that the Protestant emphasis upon man's sinfulness, upon the necessity of justification by faith, and upon the impossibility of mundane perfection is realistic, considering the facts of human existence. To the leaders of the theological revival, in our age of disaster, there has returned the tragic sense of life; they see afresh the splendor and the misery of being human and of knowing good and evil.

Dr. Harold Englund, a leading Christian scholar, thinks that Protestantism may stand on the threshold of a great era of theological and doctrinal development. Certainly there exists today a larger serious public for theological writings than booksellers have known since the middle of the nineteenth century. On the paperback racks of any good bookshop, works of theology and church history are more numerous every week; there are cheap editions of such scholarly books as Harnack's *Outlines of the History of Dogma,* Enslin's *Christian Beginnings,* H. Richard Niebuhr's *The Meaning of Revelation,* Troeltsch's *Christian Thought,* Tillich's *The New Being,* Cochrane's *Christianity and Classical Culture,* Whale's *The Protestant Tradition,* and scores more.

This theological revival is commonly associated with the work of Reinhold Niebuhr and H. Richard Niebuhr, and allied scholars strongly influenced by the Swiss theologian Karl Barth and by Sören Kierkegaard; and theirs surely is a very important movement, affecting most denominations. This "neoorthodox" group, however, has no monopoly of the intellectual restoration of Protestantism: liberal clergymen, and some who prefer simple orthodoxy to neoorthodoxy, also are at work repairing Christianity as a system of thought. During the past twenty or thirty years the Christian learning and eloquence of Lynn Harold Hough, George Buttrick, Henry P. Van Dusen, Bernard Iddings Bell, Joseph Sittler, and a dozen others have compelled even the harsher adversaries of Protestantism to confess that there is intellectual vigor among Protestants still. The rising generation of theologians is at least a match for the rationalists and positivists in American universities: one may take *Relativism, Knowledge, and Faith,* by Dr. Gordon Kaufman of Vanderbilt University, as a sample of their confident scholarship.

As yet the new theology affects only a minority of the Protestant clergy. And between earnest new ministers of the theological revival and the complacent congregations, sometimes there is strife. Since the early eighteenth century, most congregations have no strong relish for ministers who emphasize original sin and God's majesty, at least if the preacher really seems to think his flock ought to govern itself accordingly. For even the dedicated young pastor, the temptation is considerable to postpone the difficult task of restoring Christian doctrine and to take up instead what no one will disapprove: the newest busywork of the building fund and the men's breakfast club. Also, too many of the young pastors lack the ability to apply their seminary doctrines to the concrete problems of modern urban and suburban life. "I could tell you of young ministers who think of themselves as martyrs," Robert Fitch of the Pacific School of Religion said to me, smiling, "but whose heads are full of large undigested chunks of Karl Barth, which they don't know how to interpret." But as Dr. Carl Henry, editor of *Christianity Today*, puts it: ". . . the next revolution will come by rediscovering that divine justice is not merely a phase of mercy, but is itself an immutable perfection of God's very being." This rejection of sentimentality and the renewed awareness that God must be feared as well as loved are coming to characterize renascent, intellectually reputable Protestantism. We are witnessing a return to the principles which endowed Protestantism with its early power.

The doctrines of the seminaries cannot resolve, unaided, the crisis of Protestantism. In a recent report of the Lilly Endowment, one of the very few big foundations interested in Protestantism, there is this perceptive aside: "The passion born of the Social Gospel, so much in the forefront a generation ago, has now worn quite thin. . . . Doubtless the current rising tide of the intellectual pursuit of religion will also be found to have serious limitations. Man is seeking something more than bread and erudition."

The vast majority of nominal Protestants neither know nor care anything about the tendencies at Harvard Divinity School or Union Theological Seminary. How to restore Christianity as a way of life (rather than an intellectual system) remains a troubling conundrum.

The evangelical revival is a courageous frontal assault upon the problem. Led by Dr. Billy Graham, the new evangelists summon up methods that have been a phenomenon of American life since the Wesleys came to the colonies in the eighteenth century. In the disintegrated downtown centers of Detroit or Chicago or Cleveland, Graham and his friends still call men and women to repentance; and they have been heard by immense crowds.

But most of their followers in the cities, I suspect, are people who were reared in a mode of American life now trickling away. Many of them are displaced persons, reared in the old rural America, but caught up in the increasing centralization of American society, whose Protestantism subsists upon memories of the little white meetinghouse at the crossroads. Graham's sincere exhortations touch familiar chords in such minds. Yet, as Dr. Herberg suggests, this is the generation that is passing; and the response of a city-reared crowd will not be the same. We may be seeing the last of the great American revivals, even though the modern city-dweller's need for spiritual regeneration is not less than that of the American villager and country man of the last century. But it is hard to rouse his consciousness of the need.

Since early in the nineteenth century, the chief burden of dealing with mass populations in big cities has rested upon Roman Catholic clergy, rather than upon Protestants. Now, as the city looms enormous over all America, Protestant leaders cannot ignore the peculiar conditions and attitudes of the urban crowd. If Protestantism is to endure, the evangelical approach to Christian life somehow must be adjusted to urban habits and modes of expression.

How to apply Christian ethics to the modern mass life, the complex civil-social order of our time, is as profound a problem for Protestants as is the difficulty of shaking off personal complacency. A really vigorous religion is not a reflection of the economic and political order: on the contrary, religious faith shapes the economics, the politics, the literature, the art, and the whole culture of a civilization, when religion is healthy. Here, too, American Protestantism is seeking for new ideas and methods.

Before the First World War, and to some extent as late as the Second World War, many Protestant clergymen thought their duty was to alter society. Like Paul Tillich, they accepted some Marxist assumptions about the tendency of modern society, but hoped to prevent the coming of atheistic Communism by establishing a form of Christian socialism. This was the Social Gospel movement, preached by Walter Rauschenbusch and his friends. They intended to sweep away the evils of modern industrial society. Jesus' Kingdom, they declared, is not beyond time and this world of ours, but must be realized here and now, through the triumph of brotherly love, preceded by the political and economic reconstruction of society.

As a coherent movement, the Social Gospel is nearly extinct in America nowadays, and its principal advocates are either dead or, like Reinhold Niebuhr, have embraced less Utopian views.

Yet the ideology of the Social Gospel retains some hold upon American Protestantism, chiefly through the National Council of Churches (formerly the Federal Council of the Churches of Christ).

The Council was established in 1950 by merger with several other organizations, seeking to promote social reforms of the kind advocated by Rauschenbusch; and the Council's zeal for radical change lingers on. In part, this results from the constitution of the National Council: it is a coordinating, statistics-gathering, and conference-holding organization; it is not an agency for proselyting and can profess only the most general doctrines. Since it cannot advocate a doctrinal system, it tends toward preaching social reform.

Some years ago, the Council nearly equated communism and capitalism as rival evils—the alternative being, by implication, some sort of Christian socialism. This vexed many vestrymen and deacons, as well as ministers, and for more than a decade a controversy has smouldered between the officers of the Council and the leaders, often businessmen, of lay organizations. In 1955 the National Lay Committee of the National Council of Churches was dissolved primarily because the laymen, under the leadership of J. Howard Pew, had dissented vigorously from the political pronouncements of the National Council's officers.

The sort of activity to which many businessmen and other laymen objected in the Council's program is best suggested by the utterances of the National Council's World Order Study Conference, which was conducted at Cleveland for several years. In 1953, this study conference condemned the proposed Bricker Amendment to the Constitution of the United States, which would have specified that treaties must not supersede acts of Congress or the Constitution itself. The *Outlook* (now defunct), an official publication of the National Council, declared editorially, "The churches have spoken at Cleveland and through them we believe God spoke." Many Protestant clergymen protested that though the study conference claimed to speak for God, it did not speak for them. More recently, in 1958, this World Order Study Conference passed a resolution demanding that the Communist regime in China be recognized by the United States and be admitted to the United Nations. The controversy roused by this action—which was represented in many newspapers as somehow the voice of official Protestantism—still echoes through the Protestant churches.

This wistful hankering after the Social Gospel, which lingers in other places as well as among some leaders in the National Council, ought not to be put down as Communist influence or even fellow-traveling. A survey of ministers' opinions published by *Christianity Today* estimates, on the basis of "barometer questions" that 2 percent of the Protestant clergy today are communist in economic sympathies—"fellow-travelers," that is; and 25 percent are more or less socialistic. Actually this means that more Protestant ministers are more conservative in their economic opinions than they were a decade ago, and more conservative than the American population in general.

That there is a reaction against the political sermonizing of the Social Gospel period may be a sign of Protestantism's health. The Protestant churches seem to be turning once more to the primary task of the Christian religion: the ordering of souls. This task, if successfully carried out, will be reflected in an improved social order.

The social questions now plaguing America are not the problems of poverty which Rauschenbusch dealt with, nor of the decaying capitalism which Tillich predicted. Probably the most important and difficult problem plaguing Americans nowadays is the preservation of personality. For Christians, a human being is not a unit, but a unique *person*, with an immortal soul. Effectual means for enabling the person to maintain himself morally against the overweening state and the materialism of the twentieth century are being thought of as the rightful primary concern of Protestant churches in 1965, so far as the civil social order is concerned.

This altered approach to social questions is suggested by the work of Dean Robert Fitch at the Pacific School of Religion. In 1925, the year in which Fundamentalism triumphed in the Scopes trial at Dayton, Tennessee, Fitch left the Presbyterian Church in disgust. "I even canceled my membership in the Christian church," he says. "I found myself a new church, the Socialist Party, and a new religion, the philosophy of John Dewey." Since then he has worked his way back to a thorough repudiation of doctrinaire socialism and of Dewey, and to a reaffirmation of the truth of Christian doctrine. As a teacher of social ethics, Fitch spends much of his time trying to persuade political liberals of the necessity for religious foundations to social justice. Voices like his are establishing a new understanding of social problems among intelligent Protestants, wholly different from the sentimental or hypocritical attitudes caricatured in Sinclair Lewis' *Elmer Gantry*.

Of the Protestant leaders with whom I conversed, perhaps the majority felt that Dr. Marty was correct in saying that America is entering a post-Protestant era. Some think that this condition may be a salutary stimulus to Protestant convictions. Christianity often is at crisis; and often the church grows stronger in adversity. It would be better for congregations to shrink by half, several ministers told me, if by this attrition a really energizing faith could be generated among the remnant.

To sustain the Protestant concepts of self-reliance and independent personality in a standardizing milieu; to remind man that God has not really been supplanted by a computing machine; to effect a high reconciliation of traditional faith with scientific understanding —these are challenges that demand all the intellectual and emotional power that Protestantism manifested in its formative years. If the twentieth-century Protestant churches can accomplish this work, they rightly may account themselves thriving, though they no longer constitute an unofficial "established church" for America.

Of the sixty-three million Protestants, not very many have experienced the burning consciousness of justification by faith, nor have many grasped the doctrine of the exacting priesthood of all believers. Yet these principles may stir again with life. The minister in Robert Frost's poem, *The Black Cottage,* reminds us that a creed endures in truth, though ridiculed or forgotten for generations:

> Cling to it long enough, and not a doubt
> It will turn true again, for so it goes.
> Most of the change we think we see in life
> Is due to truths being in and out of favour.
> As I sit here, and oftentimes, I wish
> I could be monarch of a desert land
> I could devote and dedicate forever
> To the truths we keep coming back and back to.

Once upon a time, Protestants were folk who boldly affirmed their faith. For some while past, however, many have been folk who mildly confided their incertitudes. In several aspects modern Protestantism looks dessicated; but dry bones may rise again. "And he said unto me, Prophesy unto these bones, and say unto them, O ye dry bones, hear the word of the Lord." Thus it was with Ezekiel, in the dark days of Israel.

Whether twentieth-century Protestantism can find its prophets, able to speak with authority upon the afflictions of the mass age, no one could tell me. Yet I find evidences that American Protestants are beginning to make headway against what Santayana called "the running tide of our prosperity and triviality." America's Protestant roots go down deep.

Lenin and
the Naked Ladies

*I*n the Chicago Loop is a bookshop called Romaine's, which has its counterparts by the score in New York and Los Angeles. Its windows are adorned with Marilyn Monroe calendars, cheek by jowl with the *Collected Works of Lenin*. If you enter, you find a good many books of all sorts: but Romaine's specialities—when last I passed that way—were party-line Marxism and pornography.

One encounters an impressive variety of communist books and pamphlets, and a yet more notable variety of erotic books and naughty pictures. For the reader who takes his pornography seriously, Romaine's has case upon case of "Scarce Erotica" behind glass doors; for the neophyte or vulgarian in these studies, however, there is a cozy corner lined with little magazines devoted to Frenchwomen in the altogether. I never have been able to decide whether Romaine's intends to corrupt the politics of pornographers or the morals of Communists.

While I delectated between *Das Kapital* (abridged) and *Justine* (unexpurgated), a man of business bearing a shiny new briefcase entered the shop. He being the Man in the Gray Flannel Suit to a nicety, I marked his progress. Would Romaine's enjoy some success in seducing the business community to Stalinism? But no: making straight for Nudity Nook, he browsed briefly and then presented some pictorial Fifi in the buff to the sultry and taciturn young woman (straight out of a *New Yorker* cartoon) who sat at the cash register. Having bought his weekly quota of naked ladies, Gray Flannel trotted out of the shop, not even glancing at the back numbers of *Masses and Mainstream.*

Now this conjunction of political totalism and moral license caused me to reflect on certain censorial matters. I am not the first to observe the propinquity of Marx and Monroe. At the hearings of the Senate subcommittee looking into the scope of Soviet activities in the United States, a few years ago, this subject was raised. Mr. Philip Foner, a partner in Citadel Books and Remainder Books, was brought to testify before the subcommittee, then presided over by Senator Arthur V. Watkins. It appeared that Mr. Foner had long been associated with Communists and communist schools and publishing ventures. His firm of Citadel Books had published many Communist authors and quasi-communist volumes; also it had published many titles of a sort which Mr. Foner preferred to call "psychiatric discussions of sex." Gorki's *Mother* and Mirabeau's *Torture Garden* adorned the same list.

But what is more interesting, Mr Foner had been (through his other firm, Remainder Books) a close associate of Samuel Roth, previously sentenced to five years' imprisonment for mailing obscene publications; and Mr. Foner had been named in the Roth indictment as a co-conspirator. When questioned about this little deal, Mr. Foner took refuge behind the Fifth Amendment. Philip Foner is himself an author—the editor, among other things, of the *Collected Works of Thomas Paine.* He has also written lives—from one point of view—of Washington, Jefferson, Lincoln, and F. D. R.

The activities of persons like Mr. Foner, and the existence of more than one bookshop like Romaine's, have caused some people to wonder whether the Lenin-Fifi juxtaposition is purely coincidental. It has been suggested in *Counterattack* and elsewhere that the proven Communist traffic in Asiatic narcotics may be paralleled by an equally subtle American Communist traffic in pornography. One way to wean the people from their old opiate religion may be to provide them with the new opiate of smut; or, perhaps, it may be found convenient to prove capitalistic states morally decadent by providing them with the paraphernalia of decadence. A case can be made.

Yet that case is not easy to prove beyond a reasonable doubt. For one thing, the orthodox, hard core Communist bookshop does not traffic in pornography at all. Another favorite resort of mine in Chicago is the Modern Bookshop, situated in decent obscurity high up in a Loop office building (unlike Romaine's, which beckons popular custom from a broad window on a busy street). The Modern Bookshop is austerely serious; in place of the sultry girl-cashier, there is a civil working-class intellectual wearing (honestly) a red flannel shirt; and nothing off-color is permitted to soil the neat shelves. This is a bookseller's model bookshop, and I have been a bookseller. Every Communist book, pamphlet, and magazine in print seems to be kept in stock, and I was flattered to find one of my own works conspicuously displayed: my long essay *The Death of Art*, only so honored, I fear, for it is bound up in the same covers with Ehrenburg's *The Thaw*. There is no conservatively inclined bookshop in all this country so systematically and thoroughly devoted to a cause as is the Modern Bookshop. This little shop, indeed, is almost a museum piece, a survival from the happy days of the Popular Front; and I thought of the night the old nostalgia burned down. Nowhere did sex rear its coy head.

The Modern Bookshop and Romaine's come straight out of the pages of *1984*: the Modern established for Party members, Romaine's for the proles. The Party, in its fashion, is all things to all men. Whether the Party—as in *1984*—maintains a special bureau to produce pornographic publications, I cannot say; I doubt it, however. Almost certainly it is cheaper to purchase wholesale on the free market and retail profitably the mass production smut of Old Devil Free Enterprise. And whatever the antecedents and intentions of Mr. Foner and Mr. Roth, I am assured on good authority that the great majority of American pornographic publishers are fine up-standings 100 percent Americans, dedicated to the preservation of the most rugged individualism. The Soviets had best stick to producing jets, at which they are said to do very well; we freedom-loving liberal democrats can undersell and outproduce them ten times over when it comes to dirty magazines. And our product is much slicker than theirs. *Confidential* shouldered its way up past the *Saturday Evening Post*'s newsstand circulation; and *Playboy*, with its twoscore imitators, provides every pimply young American with the very glossiest impudicity for seventy-five cents. Don't tell us free enterprise is doomed by the resolution of thesis and antithesis: we've developed the sure-combustion formula for cheap and easy lubric-ity, available at nominal cost to the underprivileged. That formula is three bare bosoms, two pages of hoary dirty jokes, one old Somerset Maugham story, and one new Nelson Algren story; and call it the monthly *All-American Fun.* Let the Russians have their new tanks: we've got pictures of undressed trulls in five colors. We Americans feel free, and (as a young woman in California says who heads a dirty-picture-by-mail company) "we believe in the right of persons of mature mind to choose their own reading-matter."

So if the Communists are trying to gnaw at the foundations of society by selling us Mam'selle Fifi, they're wasting their time and money; we're geared to corrupt ourselves four or five times as fast as the Russians can contrive to corrupt us. Many Communists—most, probably—are somewhat archaic, still enacting the dramas of the twenties; so it remains just possible that they actually are endeavor-ing to corrupt the politics of pornographers. But there are more convincing explanations of the Lenin-Monroe axis, the union of Khrushchev with Ekberg.

There is the obvious profit motive, never ignored by practical Communists: one way to support a Communist bookshop is to put in a line of fast-selling dirty books, building the glories of the new society out of the dregs of the old. You can't find one American in ten thousand who'll read even Howard Fast (before his apostasy), but the Man in the Gray Flannel Suit fills the till at Romaine's after a brief and shamefaced browse through Nudity Nook.

And there is the old alliance, in certain types of character, between political intransigency and moral intransigency. In de Sade, Jacobinism and erotic flagellation were natural bedfellows: the impulse to destroy convention, to defile the past, moved in parallel channels. Thus, to many Communists, "bourgeois politics" and "bourgeois morality" are equally detestable, ancient iniquities deserving of any outrage. I do not mean that such is the attitude of all revolutionaries, or of all Communist revolutionaries: on the contrary, a kind of burlesque Puritanism is predominant at the commencement of most radical revolutions of this century, and many of the inner circle—like the managers and patrons of the Modern Bookshop, like the faithful Party members of *1984*—maintain an austerity in matters erotic which is a kind of caricature of Christian chastity, just as much in Communist doctrine is a caricature of Christian dogma. Nevertheless, for a large number of professed Marxists, the destruction of established moral convictions is more attractive than the hazy and distant classless society; and among the number of these, I suspect, are Romaine's and Mr. Foner and his associates.

And what ought we to do about all this? About the sale of Communist publications, I think we need to do nothing. I am not arguing from the premise of what is called "disintegrated liberalism"; I am not under the illusion that we are morally obliged to tolerate persons who would never tolerate us. The question, rather, is one of prudence. If Communist publications actually seemed to be subverting our society, then we ought to suppress them out of hand. The Bill of Rights, it cannot be said too often, is no suicide pact. But there exists no clear and present danger to us from these publications, nor even a fairly remote danger that I can discern. For Americans in this century simply will not read treatises on political and economic theory. So far as Communist propaganda is concerned, we are sheltered by our own Philistinism. And most of us never will be caught in the Communist net: we have seen too much of the consequences. If ever radicalism triumphs among us, it will be no exotic ideology; at the worst, it will have to be sugar-coated by Howard Fast and Philip Foner before we swallow the bolus; we are immune to pure doctrine of the party-line sort. Nowadays we Americans are very like the English laborer with whom Coleridge (become a Tory) argues concerning Parliamentary reform. The philosopher declared that the premises of reform led to the excesses of the French Revolution. "Damn all foreign notions!" cried the laborer. "What has the French Revolution to do with old England?" I do not think that the treatises on the shelves of the Modern Bookshop are going to outweigh the works of Mr. J. P. Marquand and Mr. Herman Wouk.

But as for the pornography, whether sold in Communist bookshops or in capitalist bookshops, I think we ought to take some prudent action. I have no notion that the dirty pictures will subvert our constitutions. Yet the dirty pictures can subvert our culture, quite measurably; they can corrupt morals and taste and the whole realm of imagination and wonder. Such publications sometimes may contribute to the increase of certain types of crime; but that is not the greatest harm they do. The debauchery of minds and sentiments by a steady diet of gross sensuality is an unmistakable mark of the decadence of any society. Every people has always had its censors, whether those censors worked through persuasion or compulsion. And an attempt to abolish even a voluntary and prudent censorship can only end—and that in quite short order—in a reaction which will produce a compulsory and imprudent censorship.

And when we have to take a stand against the girlie photographs and the sadist books, we ought not to fall into the cant of disintegrated liberalism; we ought not to indulge in impassioned defenses of prosperous pornographers upon premises which were intended to sustain the freedom of theological and political discussion. Mr. Foner's political publications may take a tentative shelter under the shadow of the *Areopagitica*, but not Mr. Foner's and Mr. Roth's erotic publications. Milton would have clapped Mr. Roth in jail as surely as Napoleon clapped de Sade in the lunatic asylum.

Despite all the talk about "the threat to the freedom to read," the only really serious threat to reading in this country comes from the apathy of Americans when confronted with any sort of book. A boy I know reports that in his town, the only people he ever finds in the public library are old ladies posting placards about the threat to the freedom to read. Now and then, of course, we are visited by some silliness about books on library shelves; but that sort of silliness is one of the inevitable prices of democracy, and it comes as often from liberal zealots as from conservative zealots. We are perfectly free to read anything we like; but we choose to read almost nothing.

No really powerful group in this country desires to interfere with the publication and the purchase of works on theology or politics or any other serious subject. It might be well enough for book reading if some power really *did* oppose on principle the freedom to read: then we Americans might begin to suspect there is something inside books after all. What the seventeenth- and eighteenth- and nineteenth-century champions of a free press never expected was our present American condition: a state of almost perfect freedom to print and distribute whatever one may choose and a coexisting almost complete indifference to serious books on the part of the general public.

So I do not indulge the dread that in locking up Mr. Roth, or in questioning Mr. Foner, we may betray the Bill of Rights, the legacy of John Stuart Mill, or any other liberties cherished by the orator. I do not think that we need to padlock the Modern Bookshop, or that we will do anything of the sort. I do not propose to snatch that set of Lenin out of Romaine's window. But if anyone tells me that my local druggist has an inalienable right to sell printed nastiness (at a cheering profit) to ninth-grade boys, I shall reply that any right may be alienated through abuse. Any civilized community has its pre-scriptive rights, thoroughly legitimate. And one of those prescriptions is the right to abate a stench.

WEALTH AND CULTURE

The Inhumane
Businessman

*T*aken in the gross, American men of business are inhumane. I do not mean that they are inhuman; they are all too human. I do not mean that they are insufficiently humanitarian; on the contrary, many of them have embraced too enthusiastically the creed of the sentimental humanitarian. But I do mean just this: American merchants and industrialists, like most other Americans, are deficient in the disciplines which nurture sound imagination and strong moral character. They do not know the arts of *humanitas,* which teach a man his true nature and his duties.

Humanism, succinctly defined, is the belief that man is a distinct being, governed by laws peculiar to his nature; there is law for man and law for thing. The humanities form that body of studies which, through acquaintance with great literature, teach the capabilities and the limitations of human nature.

As Irving Babbitt wrote half a century ago, nowadays the word humanism "is equally on the lips of the socialistic dreamer and the exponent of the latest philosophical fad." But really the humanist is a man who, in Matthew Arnold's phrase, sees life steadily and sees it whole. He recognizes the supernatural and the natural world, and tries to harmonize the claims of both in his own life and in society. Possessing what we awkwardly call "a well-rounded mind" and "a well-balanced personality," he believes in proportion, harmony, moderation. He is a many-sided man; and he is not easily led into excess, for he possesses some sound knowledge of a good many subjects. In order to understand what the humane attitude means, Babbitt wrote, "we may borrow a homely illustration from the theory of commercial crises. A minority of men may be prudent and temper their enterprise with discretion, but the majority is sure to over-trade, and so unless restrained by the prudent few will finally bring on themselves the nemesis of a panic."

In business and in the whole of life, then, our humanist is a man who takes long views. By virtue of his fund of sound knowledge, he can predict with fair accuracy the consequences of actions. Because he has a disciplined mind, he is temperate; because he knows the greatness and the weakness of human character, he is prudent.

I do not say that the American businessman is worse, or better, in his acquaintance with humane learning than are other orders of Americans. My immediate concern is that in our "business civilization," in our practical politics which radicals call "business rule," the American businessman is ill equipped for intellectual and political leadership. The humane disciplines were developed in considerable part to train the leaders of a nation. In our time, businessmen necessarily are leaders. If those businessmen are inhumane, they are incompetent as leaders and incomplete as men.

Now the humanist is not identical with the humanitarian. "Humanitarianism" involves one of three beliefs, or a combination of the three: (1) that Jesus Christ possessed a human nature only, not a divine nature; (2) that mankind may be perfected without divine aid; (3) and that benevolence or philanthropy constitutes the whole of man's duties. As Professor Eric Voegelin points out in *The New Science of Politics,* this doctrine we call humanitarianism has done infinite mischief in the modern world. There exist among us a great many humanitarians; most of them are grossly sentimental, and many of them are businessmen. But that is another matter, for just now I am writing about humane disciplines.

In cant journalism, "humanitarian" has come to mean a philanthropist. Like most other people, I heartily approve of philanthropists—so long as those philanthropists do not hold that mere indiscriminate giving can substitute for mental and moral disciplines, or take the place of good constitutions and prescriptive laws. In philanthropy the American businessman certainly has not been found wanting: with the possible exception of the merchants and manufacturers and bankers of nineteenth-century England, no class of businessmen in all history has been so openhanded and so tender in "social conscience" as our twentieth-century American businessmen. Sometimes, indeed, our businessmen have been imprudently zealous for mere material benefactions. I do not mean that the American man of business is selfish—only that he is inhumane.

The truly humane person is one who knows that we were not born yesterday. Acquainted with the great books and the great lives of the past, and with the best thought of his own generation, he has received the benefits of a truly liberal education, a training of mind and character which chastens and ennobles and emancipates. Though a man genuinely free, he enjoys liberty only because he obeys the ancient laws that govern human nature. Whether in his own little circle or on the national scale, he is competent to lead—to lead in thought and taste and politics—because he has served an apprenticeship to the priests and prophets and philosophers of the generations which have preceded him. He knows what it is to be a man, truly and fully human. He knows his rights and his duties. He knows what to do with his leisure. He knows the purpose of his work. He knows that there exists law for man and law for thing.

Ever since the Hebrew prophets began to describe the rules which govern man as man, under God, and ever since the glory that was Greece began to shine, certain strict and exacting disciplines have existed to humanize men, to educate the leaders of a people. Cicero and Seneca and Marcus Aurelius were at once the Roman exemplars and the Roman preceptors of this humanizing process which we refer to as "a liberal education." It was found that through the study of great lives and great thoughts, the minds of earnest men in every generation might be moulded nobly. This process, both intellectual and ethical, was intended to develop strong and just characters through the training of strong and just intellects. Its principal tool was the "classic," the great book—especially the literature of theology, philosophy, poetic imagination, history, and biography. Homer, Plato, Aristotle, Sophocles, Thycydides, Livy, Cicero, Virgil, Plutarch, and a score of other ancient authors formed the core of this humane discipline, which came to dominate the whole of the Western world and persisted little altered in American colleges until very late in the nineteenth century. Through such means, John Henry Newman, in Discourse V of his *The Idea of a University Defined and Illustrated,* wrote, "a habit of mind is formed which lasts through life, of which the attributes are freedom, equitableness, calmness, moderation, and wisdom; of what . . . I have ventured to call the philosophical habit."

With this classical heritage, Newman and his predecessors among the great Christian humanists—Erasmus and More and the rest —combined the wealth of Jewish and Christian learning, transcendental as well as ethical in character. The model "Christian gentleman" was a leader schooled in both the classical works and Christian literature. Into the fabric of humane letters were woven the Old and New Testaments, the writings of the Fathers of the Church, the letters and sermons of the great divines, the English Book of Common Prayer. This complex fabric of education was not seriously challenged until late in the eighteenth century and was not badly injured until the middle of the nineteenth century. And it persists, however much weakened, among us still. It is difficult to exaggerate, for instance, how profoundly the young American Republic was influenced by this humane tradition. The founders of the Republic were practical and bold men; but they were also humane. Even those who had read little were exposed, from childhood, to the Bible, Cicero, Virgil, and Plutarch, if only in translation or through a kind of intellectual osmosis. The pattern for the American Republic was the Roman Republic, modified by the English political experience; the models for American leadership were Plutarch's heroes.

Until the commercial revolution transformed medieval Europe, the banker and the merchant and the manufacturer did not dominate society—though we ought not to neglect the importance of their class in the Greek states and in Rome, or in the medieval burghs. By and large, however, the leaders of society in the ancient world and the medieval world were the landed proprietors, the clergy, and the lawyers. It was these latter classes who were trained in the humane diciplines. But as the businessman commenced to attain social and political influence, he too began to enter upon humane studies.

The merchant-nobles of Venice, the great burghers of the Low Countries, the bankers of Lombardy and Tuscany, the rising manufacturers of England, the traders of the Hanse—all soon aspired to acquire knowledge of and to patronize humane letters and arts. From them, as well as from princes and nobles, the Renaissance humanists received admiration and aid. In England, the "nation of shopkeepers," the upper middle classes, in time, nearly preempted the role of guardian of culture formerly filled by church and nobility: the famous public schools, in their modern form, arose to acquaint the sons of the upper middle classes with classical and Christian learning. Even in raw America, at the periphery of the Western world, the merchants of Boston and of Charleston tried to make their seaports into a new Athens or Corinth. John Adams, in commercial Massachusetts, applied classical political experience to American exigencies. George Grote, an English banker, wrote the great nineteenth-century history of Greece.

But with the successive industrial revolutions of the nineteenth and twentieth centuries, with what Friedrich Juenger calls "the triumph of technology," this veneration of humane learning began to diminish among men of business, especially in America. Applied science seemed the key to power, possibly the cure to all the ills of humanity; the social theories grouped under the label of "positivism" provided a convenient apology for the deification of technology. With the acceleration of nearly everything in modern life, it began to seem as if higher education ought to be accelerated proportionately. Were not the humane disciplines so much dead wood? Could not we Americans get things done faster, and better, by sweeping aside all this mass of dusty learning and striding on to the immediate increase of production? Why waste years in school over the Old Testament and Cicero? In the Old Testament and in Cicero there resides little profit—of the commercial sort.

Not merely businessmen, or young people aspiring to become businessmen, talked this way: in the colleges and universities many powerful voices were raised in denunciation of the humanities and in praise of "efficiency," "pragmatism," "instrumentalism," and "modern progress." The School of Business Administration pushed into a dark and impoverished corner the School of Classical Studies. Only at a few small colleges and in some retreats in great universities, nowadays, do the old humane disciplines survive recognizably; and not one in a thousand political or industrial leaders can quote his Cicero, let alone his St. Augustine.

A civilization or a nation can keep going for a long time on the impetus given its culture by a body of ideas that have been severed from their roots. Exhausting gradually the source of their spiritual and social prosperity, a people can, without knowing their precarious condition, live upon moral and intellectual capital for generations after this capital levy, this intellectual deficit financing, has commenced.

Yet eventually such a civilization or nation arrives at cultural bankruptcy. The traditional process which produced leadership, withering as nutriment, no longer finds its way up from those severed cultural roots, ceases to function almost altogether; the intellectual and political and industrial leaders of the older generation die one by one; and their places are not filled. The humanitarian cannot do duty for the humane man. There can come only two alternative results from this withering: a social decadence from which no recovery is possible, or else a social revolution which produces radical and unscrupulous aspiring talents to turn society inside out. When all the humane leaders have vanished, a nation's only recourse for leadership is the commissar, under one name or another. That commissar is not humane: for honor and tradition, he substitutes naked power. That commissar is not philanthropic: though he may employ the jargon of the sentimental philanthropist, he settles for the great grim reward of thoroughgoing egoism, domination over the minds and the bodies of other men and women. With George Orwell's O'Brien, he has the monstrous gratification of stamping forever on a human face.

Now I think that our businessmen are philanthropic, good-natured, technologically efficient, and harmless. Most of them are even likable. I should be infinitely sorry to see them supplanted by so many commissars. But, so far as the understanding of human nature and human intellect and orderly society is concerned, most of our businessmen are babies. Though the innocence of the baby has its charms, at the switchboard the baby may be incalculably dangerous, not least to himself. Any nation has its body of leaders, determined by the nature of that people; whether we like it or not, much of the leadership of our society must be exercised by our businessmen. I do not wish to see our businessmen abolished; therefore I hope to see them humanized. I think it possible for them to grow from babies into men. That is precisely what humane education is supposed to accomplish.

"This process of training," Cardinal Newman wrote, in Discourse VII, "by which the intellect, instead of being formed or sacrificed to some particular or accidental purpose, some specific trade or profession, or study or science, is disciplined for its own sake, for the perception of its own object, and for its own highest culture, is called Liberal Education; and though there is no one in whom it is carried as far as is conceivable, yet there is scarcely any one but may gain an idea of what real training is and at least look toward it, and make its true scope, not something else, his standard of excellence."

Plenty of money has been available for a good while to provide this liberal education, this humane discipline, for aspirants to business leadership; but few really have sought it. To most, "training" has meant technological and technical accomplishments.

One anecdote: I happen to know of the middle-aged son of an eminent industrialist. A man of practical genius, the father has spent his whole life inventing, planning, and mass-producing; he has never had time for such frivolities as humane letters. The son, however, has plenty of time for anything: he has money, social position, formal schooling, and no real responsibilities. How does he employ this abundance of time? He keeps out of mischief: he goes down to his big basement and makes model steam locomotives. Thus are his days and his evenings spent, with only the occasional diversion of a cocktail party. I do not mean that he is interested in technological progress: he leaves that to the hired hands. His tiny locomotives are simply Lilliputian copies of existing, or formerly existing, engines. In his hobby there is no alloy of utility: down he goes to the cellar for fun, and in that fun his decades slip by. He is no moron; he is simply inhumane. Henry Adams wrote that the progress of our Republic from Washington to Grant refuted the theory of selective evolution. I am inclined to think that the progress of scientific technology from Francis Bacon to the model-locomotive addict refutes the theory of utilitarian education.

Were this merely an isolated instance of eccentricity, or a symptom only of an age of abundant leisure, of course we could afford to smile—and let other people get on with the world's work. But I fancy that the industrialist's aging son in his cellar is a microcosm of what our American culture is producing. When the rights and the duties that are inculcated by an humane discipline begin to be neglected in favor of an ingenuous "getting on with practical things," then the moral and intellectual and political leadership of a nation sinks into atrophy. I think that ignoring humanizing disciplines has brought us face to face with three immense problems: the harm that is done to the potential leaders; the harm that is done to business; and the harm that is done to the whole culture. Is life worth living? Every generation asks itself that question; and if the purpose of life is to construct miniature locomotives, then our generation must reply with a whispered negative.

In *A Chapter of Erie*, the younger Charles Francis Adams described the financiers and industrialists of the Gilded Age with much loathing. He had dwelt among them; after a fashion, he had been one of them. Of these businessmen, Adams said, scarcely any might be encountered with whom an educated man could carry on an interesting conversation, or whom you might care to invite to your house for dinner.

Well, the manners, the morals, and the formal instruction of our businessmen seem to have improved since the Gilded Age, and I know a good many worth talking with. But not enough. And I have observed that of the more intelligent and interesting business executives whom I have met, the majority were not trained as "industrialists" at all. My favorites, most of them, were schooled in the law: as lawyers, rather than as experts upon production or distribution or finance, they rose to leadership in great corporations.

Now although our law schools labor under a number of deficiencies, still it is certain that anyone who attends a reputable law school must know some Latin, a fair amount of history, and even a smattering of philosophy. Possibly it was not the law schools which made my industrialist friends humane, but the discipline probably helped; and at least it did not hinder their self-education in humane letters. These men had some years in which to think upon abiding truths and the procession of civilization. Many of them continue to read theology, philosophy, history, and the works of the imagination.

In spite of the obsession with getting-things-done-fast that is expected of ambitious young men in business, these gentlemen are humane.

Banking, too, still has its well-read men, though most of them seem to belong to the generation that is passing. My grandfather, a small-town banker, was one such, with his sets of Macaulay and Dickens and Mark Twain, his shelves of poetry, his considerable grasp of history, his folio of Froissart and his Gibbon in quarto. But as matters are going, we shall not long look upon this manner of man.

In banking or manufacturing or merchandizing, the rising executive now is the least leisured man in the world. Often enough he works hours which make the factory-week of the Bleak Age seem feckless. A perceptive Episcopalian clergyman tells me of how the junior executives who make up the majority of his parishioners have no time for real thought, let alone religious and civic duties; they feel, and not without reason, that they have done their whole duty by the church if they contrive to put in a drowsy appearance on Sunday mornings. By leisure, Aristotle says, a man is made wise; but the young men who are to govern our industry and influence our public polity are in the state of Aristotle's slaves, disqualified from a part in public affairs by the necessity of unremitting labor. When they are in their sixties, they may have time and energy to spare for reflection and community endeavor and public service. But there are disadvantages in being led by emancipated slaves, the freedmen of industrial production. Nor is it easy to humanize oneself, abruptly, at the age of sixty.

At the turn of the century, the chairman of the board of a large British chemical concern was J. Meade Faulkner—who also was a wonderfully talented romantic novelist. I see none such rising among us. Sherwood Anderson walked out of his own factory, in disgust, to turn to writing; to him these two occupations seemed wholly inconsonant. Nor do many of our businessmen acquire late in life a taste for humane letters: for one thing, their mortality rate is notoriously high, perhaps in part because they lack the consolations of philosophy and the relaxation of intellectual pursuits; for another, the disciplines of language and chronology and simple grounding in humane studies, so easily acquired in childhood, are thoroughly tedious in old age. "Then Tantalus' be his delight. . . ." A businessman may pursue all his days the will-o'-the-wisp of leisure; and when at length he clutches the phantom, it slips through his fingers like fog.

A friend of mine, an experienced man of business, took me for a walk through his fashionable suburb. Rather against his will, my friend had been graduated from Massachusetts Institute of Technology (M.I.T.) and Harvard Business School; also, however, he had spent some years in liberal studies at a German university, and had read broadly.[1] We passed scores of big houses, each silent as death—because all the occupants were watching television. The average of their incomes was very high. "In this whole town," my friend said, "there are perhaps three or four people who might bother to buy your book *The Conservative Mind;* and perhaps six or seven who are prepared to understand it if someone should give them a copy." Such is our class with the responsibility for patronizing culture and setting the tone of politics.

Perhaps the greatest pity is this: most of our businessmen are unaware, except in the vaguest sense, that they are missing anything. If they join the Book of the Month Club, they feel that they have done their duty by the works of the mind. For integrity and industriousness and strong intellectual powers deserve their rewards; and the highest reward of merit, in this life, is the enjoyment of liberality of mind and spirit. Whether or not it might be better to live as a pagan suckled in a creed outworn, surely a very large part of the intellectual talents of this nation are laid waste in getting and spending. In themselves, getting and spending generally are commendable activities; as Samuel Johnson said, a man is seldom more innocently occupied than when he is engaged in making money. But that efficient production and swift promotion should become the crown of life to many of the best minds and hearts in our generation

[1] Paradoxically, some of the technical colleges, most notably M.I.T., in recent years have commenced programs of humane studies that often excel those at old-fashioned liberal arts colleges: this in consequence of a growing recognition that industrialists and engineers need to be humane. Meanwhile, most liberal arts colleges, sedulous to appear progressive, have so diluted their own humane studies that what remains is the shadow of a shade. And when I professed at a big state university, I observed that of my few decently prepared students in history, many came from technical high schools and military academies, where whatever is taught in the way of languages and literature and history still is taught with unenlightened thoroughness, upon the assumption that such students never will have another whack at culture.

is seriously unjust: unjust to the businessman who never has learned to look for anything more.

To know the wonder of great poetry; to look upon the majesty of history; to become acquainted with noble lives; to have some share in the intuitions of genius; to understand something of the nature of the universe; to feel oneself a part of a living continuity and essence—these things are the real crown of life and ought to be the reward of remarkable abilities, even though those talents have been put to utilitarian ends. So far as culture is concerned, I am in favor of equal opportunity and fair shares for all. And here the businessman is miserably underprivileged, to employ a word sufficiently barbarous—itself a sign of the decay of learning among us.

Nor is his present plight irrevocable. In an age of abundant production, when for the first time in history the problems of mass leisure are more pressing—here in America and in much of western Europe—than the problems of mass production, the businessman is one of the few persons (sometimes the clergyman is in the same boat) who work harder and more singlemindedly than ever before. Nobody talks about the thirty-hour week for the businessman—who, so far as natural abilities go, probably has more to gain from true leisure than has his average employee. I am not proposing that the businessman ought to knock off in the middle of the week and enroll in an adult education course. What I am suggesting is that the schooling and the informal education of the potential man of business, in his youth, ought to cultivate in him those tastes, and equip him with those disciplines, that enable the pleasures of a humane consciousness to make their way naturally and gracefully into even the busiest career. He would live longer because of this, probably; and certainly he would live better.

If the businessman needs humane culture for his heart's ease, business needs the humane man quite as much for the sake of real efficiency. Now and then I lunch with an investment broker, a gentleman who knows his Shakespeare, Dryden, and Addison. (There were no graduate schools of business when he was young, so he spent his time reading good books, at random, and making money at an early age.) They say he has seventy millions now; but that is possibly an underestimate. Now and again he has a university president bring professors to see him, so that he may find out what they are like nowadays. Generally he finds them over specialized and dogmatic; they are not so humane as he would prefer. Once the president brought a professor of education, a genus he had not before inspected.

"Do you think," said the broker to the professor of education, "that young people are better educated now than they were in 1900?"

The professor of pedagogy did indeed think so: ever so much better educated; integrated with the group, adjusted to the environment, and benefiting from curricular enrichments. "I am glad to hear it," the broker remarked. "I had wondered about it, because when I bring young men into my office I generally find that they cannot write decent letters, or understand an alphabetical filing-system."

At its lower levels, our difficulty is as simple as that: the neglect of the old educational disciplines, in favor of socialization and specialization, to such a point that it is not easy to get the world's work done. Someone has to think, even with automation; someone has to write and file. To expect a business to teach its clerks the alphabet is to carry on-the-job training rather far.

One learns how to write decent letters through having to read a few books in decent English. The attempt of the colleges to temper the old humanities to "the needs of a business civilization" actually has worked mischief for business firms. When I was an undergraduate, a dean recommended to me that I enroll in a course in "business letter writing," for which full credit was given—as part of the humanities curriculum. This might be substituted for a course (presumably vexatious to any up-and-coming student) in Greek myth or a course in Browning, either of which I had considered taking. Any office manager knows that a literate typist who never before had done a day's commercial work can master the peculiarities of business correspondence with ten minutes of diligent application. But it is not possible to master Hesiod or *The Ring and the Book* in ten months of application, if one has no humane schooling. The inhumane dean and the inhumane professor have some share in the shame of the inhumane businessman.

But the importance of humane disciplines to the functioning of industry and commerce is greater than the mere mastery of simple literacy skills. One of the ends of a liberal education is to fit a person for whatever lot may happen to be his; and some of the accomplishments of the humane disciplines, though that system of learning developed in an age considerably different from ours, are remarkably important to the management of modern economy.

For one thing, a person truly educated in the humane tradition has an orderly mind—so far as any system of training can bring order into personality. He has been taught the relationships between cause and effect; he is accustomed to taking long views. He expects certain consequences to follow from certain actions. He has in his mind a fund of precedent. He is acquainted with system, respects just authority, and has been told that the ego must be kept in check. These intellectual acquirements are adapted easily enough to the exigencies of modern business, which in its complexity requires precisely those habits of thought and action that a liberal education has been inculcating in man these several centuries.

Such a person tends also to exercise creative imagination. The variety of ideas which he has explored, the metaphysical and critical concepts with which he has grown familiar, the poetic invention that he has enjoyed, all give to the humanely schooled man a resourcefulness often lacking in the man trained only technically. To the liberal intellect occur the larger possibilities; while technique, per se, often breeds only refinements of existing techniques. Most definitely the humanely educated is not William H. Whyte's "organization man," which makes him less amenable, perhaps, to commands from on high; yet no firm composed principally of "organization men" in high posts can live for many years, unless it is something close to a monopoly. Big publishing houses have collapsed because of the predominance of "organization men" over humane intellects. Imagination rules the world, Napoleon said. Though business imagination is not the highest form of creative intellect, certainly it rules business, in a competitive economy.

I suggest yet another advantage of the humane intellect in business: that it is in some sort a promise and guarantee of integrity. The end of the old humanistic schooling was ethical: to teach a man virtue through knowledge of important books and important lives. Of course there are dishonest men of humane acquirements. But the possession of a humanely disciplined mind creates a legitimate presumption in favor of a man's integrity.

After some years of reading the philosophers, prophets, and poets, a man at least must be ashamed of misconduct, even though he gives way to it. It is a Latin poet who tells us that a man may perceive the good path and the evil, and yet choose the evil almost against his will, and surely against his reason; there are no absolute sureties against a fall from virtue. But a man who knows that both good and evil exist seems a trustier prospect than an operator like Willis Wayde, who is almost totally unaware that he ever had done anything unethical. Upon trust we build the complex fabric of our industrial and financial order; no previous economic system ever depended upon faith and habitual integrity as does ours. Dr. Johnson, on being told of a neighbor who maintained that there exists no distinction between virtue and vice, said only, "Why, then, let us count our spoons when he leaves." Where the humane tradition prevails, with its emphasis upon honor, there is less need for spoon-counting.

And one last suggestion as to the general traits inculcated by humane disciplines: liberal education helps a man to know his fellows. It cannot substitute for native shrewdness and familiarity with the ways of the world, but it can supplement and elevate such worldly wisdom. The humanely educated man knows a good deal about human hopes and motives, from his study of imaginative literature, biography, and history. He is not liable to mistake his own preferences for universal aspirations or to repose a utopian faith in his associates. He probably has taken on a healthy pessimism about the possibilities of human nature. He knows fairly well what may be expected of the average sensual man, and what may not.

He does not have to go weekly to the analyst for treatment of his psyche, if he is fairly normal. He may have taken to heart the Delphic maxim, "Nothing in excess." Now such a person has some preparation for dealing with the difficulties of "personnel relations"; he has a better training, I am inclined to believe, than the young zealot fresh from courses in Freudian or behavioristic psychology, applying immoderately the speculations of the clinician to situations and personalities that may require nothing more than a sprinkling of good humor.

Yet despite these merits of the humanely disciplined mind in business, doors have been closing for a long while in business and industry against the "liberal arts graduate." In part, this results from the lamentable attitude of certain businessmen, often themselves unacquainted with the inside of colleges, who think of all education as training and therefore expect to employ trained people for narrow specialties. And in part, this is the fault of educational adminis-trators who have pandered to "the needs of industry" by setting up wondrously technical or even manual curricula—expecting subsidies and gifts from business by way of reward. One state university now offers a four-year curriculum in packaging, leading to the degree of bachelor of science in packaging. There may be fine opportunities in the back room of Woolworth's for these bachelors of science.

As things are going, one professor says, his university soon will be offering a curriculum in alligator stuffing. This silly and damaging specialization extends beyond the needs of industry: the university with the packaging curriculum also offers courses, with credit, in fly-casting. All this is described by college presidents as "serving the needs of the community." A community, or an industry, which actually makes such demands upon colleges is liable in short order to become an impoverished community or industry. "There is nothing to which we will not stoop," says the president of a famous state university, "if the public seems to demand it." But the businessman with any concern for the future of business or of the nation ought to set his face against these absurdities, rather than applauding their proliferation.

Already, indeed, one may find encouraging signs that intelligent men of business are turning against college pandering of this sort. In England, a decade ago, the chairman of Imperial Chemical Industries announced that he did not desire to employ any more "industrial specialists" and "public relations personnel" and "personnel-relations technicians" sprung fully armed from the brow of the university. What he wanted was young men with a humane education, able to turn their minds to a wide variety of tasks. Some American executives have made statements nearly as vigorous —though they have not always acted upon their own pronunciamentos. And the junior executives who have suffered under the domination of college specialization are turning against their own muddled training. A relative of mine with a chemical engineering degree, now in the Persian oil fields, has done well at his post —but not from anything he got out of his college courses other than the standard liberal arts and scientific studies. His favorite author is Plutarch, and he learns more about managing men from the *Lives of the Noble Greeks and Romans* than ever he learned from Industrial Psychology 301.

One day Johnson and Boswell went boating on the Thames in a wherry, and Johnson playfully asked the wherry boy what he would give to learn Greek. He had very little money, said the wherry boy, but he would give all he had; this pleased Samuel Johnson mightily. A little of that longing for humane letters is creeping back into our rising generation, and, unlike Johnson's wherry boy, we are able to afford to pay for it. Cheerfulness will keep breaking in. "Experience is a hard teacher," wrote that eminently successful businessman Ben Franklin, "but fools will have no other." From harsh experience, if from nothing else, American business may be awakening to the consequences of dehumanized work and schooling.

For the body politic, businessmen are not the ideal leaders. Edmund Burke, it is true, included among the natural aristocracy of a nation "rich traders, who from their success are presumed to have sharp and vigorous understandings, and to possess the virtues of diligence, order, constancy, and regularity, and to have cultivated an habitual regard to commutative justice." [2] Yet Burke—though for a time he sat in the House of Commons for Bristol, then the chief commercial center of England, and was supported always by the greater part of the industrial and commercial interests—did not trust the businessman as a statesman; on another occasion he said that men of commerce were not at all fit to judge of the high concerns of state. And a distinguished politician even more heartily endorsed by the business community than was Burke, Robert Taft, more than once expressed his annoyance at the notion that the United States needed a "businessman's government": businessmen, he said, should take care of business, and politicians should take care of politics.

These persuasive opinions notwithstanding, the businessman matters in American politics, and must continue to matter, whether he likes it or not. Many businessmen definitely do not like it; by definition, they are busy, and they know when they are out of their element.

Against the overweening political ambition of the capitalist, radical publicists still warn us; but in truth ambition should be made of sterner stuff. We suffer far more from the political indifference of the businessman than from his alleged aspiration to an hegemony. One night a friend of mine pointed out an enormous neon sign atop an office building, of dubious advertising value but of indubitable hideousness. "That sign cost fifty thousand dollars," my friend said, "deductible from taxes as a cost of doing business, of course; most of the money would have been taken by the government, otherwise. The man who put it up wouldn't give ten dollars if he were offered a chance to save the Republic."

[2] Edmund Burke, *An Appeal from the New to the Old Whigs* (1791).

No, our businessman is not the perfect statesman; but no matter how much he and we might like to amend matters, he will have to be concerned with our public polity. Whoever possesses money and influence plays the principal role in the nation's politics, or else he does not retain money and influence long. We possess no large class of landed proprietors to pass our laws and carry on our administration, such as existed in England until quite recently. Nor have we anything very like the professional and old-school-tie aristocracy that still has much to do with the government of Britain. We do have some men of private means, not themselves engaged in business, like Taft and Stevenson and Harriman and Rockefeller, who exercise a real influence. But these are not numerous enough to constitute a governing class. The amorphous character of party organization, or lack of organization, in this country tends to thrust political responsibility back upon private individuals and local groups the moment a national election is over. Even though our businessman is not the complete statesman, he must continue to be in politics so long as he continues to be in business—and this is the more true as government intervenes increasingly in the functioning of the economy. Politics is the art of the possible; and it is vain to hope that anyone will emerge to relieve the businessman from this burden. We can hope only to improve the businessman as an arbiter of politics.

Here the businessman without humane disciplines is most conspicuously found wanting. If ignorant of history and political theory and the record of human nature, but well intentioned and philanthropic, often he falls victim to the sentimental humanitarian or, worse still, to the power-craving zealot for doctrinaire political alteration. Vaguely eager to be approved by the "Advanced Social Thinker," such a well-meaning inhumane businessman becomes a party to his own undoing: which might be tolerated, were it not that his order, and the economy of which he is symbol and product, are bound up inextricably with the Republic's welfare and the civilization we enjoy. The radical proponent of a Utopian society is quite aware of this weakness of the inhumane businessman, and he acts accordingly. More than a generation gone, an American man of letters who happened to be an ardent socialist, G. Lowes Dickinson, informed his friends that they could count upon the conquest of businessmen and the like without a struggle: a "slow, half-conscious detachment of all of them who have intelligence and moral force from the interest and active support of their class."

In this fashion the Fabians set to work in England; and the process has been discernible in the United States for some years, though no organization so clever and compact as the Fabian Society has appeared to hasten it. In both England and America, the socialist millionaire is a common enough figure. To play upon a confused feeling of family or personal guilt among the rich—to denounce the Robber Barons and, in the next breath, to praise their grandsons who have set their steps in another path; to cajole and threaten in turn—such are the tactics of the collectivist. The deficits of the radical weeklies are met dutifully by the social-conscience-ridden capitalist. Now in their day the robber barons did some damage; but the possibilities are greater far for damage to our social structure by the confused and sentimental benefactions of Humanitarian Barons.[3]

We have, then, the inhumane businessman who is supinely indifferent to political theory and political action and the inhumane businessman who is easily seduced to the cause of fallacious political action; and there is a third type. This third sort seems to me better than the other two, though he is not without fault.

I mean the inhumane businessman who blunders manfully, generously, clumsily into practical politics, intending to defend his own interests and the public interest, but woefully ill-prepared to accomplish an effectual defense. Not every man is a proper champion of the truth, says old Sir Thomas Browne; many there are who have rashly charged the troops of Error and fallen trophy to the enemy. Every national administration has had its quota of these valorous Quixotes, smug in a few political dogmas and slogans, uttering speeches written by public relations experts in their twenties,

---

[3] The policies of a number of our great private charitable foundations also are intimately affected by an imprudent reaction against "rugged individualism." Yesterday's abuse is not atoned for by today's blunder. In general, most of the big foundations are committed—not to collectivism, as their adversaries complain—but to a vague, well-intentioned humanitarianism, looking toward the perfection of society and human nature and sinning more by waste of funds than by any positively baneful policies. Almost any sum of money can be obtained for almost any "social-science research" scheme, or plan for material amelioration; almost no money can be found for any proposal for humane studies. Our foundations have a great deal for the body, or for the social scientist, but little for the mind. The lack of humane education among their founders and directors has something to do with this; and the peculiar and novel class of foundational "organization men" which is growing up among us seems ignorant, taken as a group, of the ethical and intellectual premises that form the humane tradition.

confident in the "American way of life" and the "American standard of living," doing mischief to their allies at home and their allies abroad by imprudence of speech and unpredictability of action. For such a representative inhumane businessman, history began at his own birth, or in his adolescence; and so foreign policy is to be determined not by a subtle understanding of the passions and prejudices and interests of the nations, over the long run, but merely by references to "what Hitler did in 1940" and to "what the Arab people want." Literature, to such a representative inhumane businessman, is current periodicals, particularly those that employ only short paragraphs; and so the great principles of morality and prudent statecraft are deduced from the vaticinations of the syndicated columnist. Ascent to high place in society, Burke says, should not be made too easy: quick success breeds presumption. Some of our businessmen have gone straight to the top in twenty or thirty years. But the talents which made possible such a triumph are not easily translated into the governance of the state, if humane learning is lacking.

In state governments and in the national government, and locally, we retain a saving remnant of humane businessmen concerned with politics; and I do not know what we should do without them. We ought not to try to expel the businessman from political leadership; we ought only to persuade him to look into Sir Thomas Elyot's *Boke Called the Governour*. Elyot, a humanist, knew that a humane discipline is an education for governors, for the just leaders without whom the commonwealth perishes. Without such an education, it is scarcely possible for the best-intentioned and most soundly inclined politician to act righteously. Any nation must take its leaders where it can find them. From among the businessmen we must take many of ours.

I do not think we can delay much longer in the restoration of learning among men of business. If they fail to lead, other leaders, of a disagreeable and violent stamp, will make themselves felt in the land. Burke described Jacobinism, the fierce radicalism of France, as "the revolt of the enterprising talents of a country against its property." Jacobinism lies latent in any generation or nation. If neither the possessors of property nor the enterprising talents are chastened by the councils of true humanism, it will be of no avail simply to mutter, like incantations, slogans about "the essential rightness of a democratic society."

To exhort the American businessman to practice the high old Roman virtue may seen sufficiently ludicrous. Yet the hard-headed and conscientious American man of business is not altogether unlike the old Roman citizen. If the American businessman had any inkling of what the old Roman stood for, he might be fortified in this time of troubles by the Roman *humanitas,* which Cicero represented at its best. *Pietas* and *officium* governed the lives of the men who upheld the Roman Republic: piety and duty. To be either pious or dutiful is very difficult, unless one has some grasp of the legacy of civilization; and human learning is the means by which we come to understand that legacy.

If only by accident, the American businessman has come to be a chief guardian of our civil and cultural inheritance. To have greatness thrust upon one is not always pleasant. Yet the American businessman seems to owe it to himself, his economic system, and his country to shoulder such responsibilities. I do not expect that any considerable proportion of the business community will set out overnight to read Plato through or to look upon beauty bare. Yet if only one percent of our men of business were to begin to pay some heed to the springs of imagination and reason, we might give the lie to the European witticism that America is the only nation to pass from barbarism to decadence without knowing civilization.

The Indispensable
Patron

*E*verything has to be paid for, even truth and beauty. Every
civilization worth calling a civilization has its patrons of arts and
letters who foot the bills. Among the indices to the quality of any
culture, the taste and generosity of those patrons must stand high.

Religion being the great source of thought and art, in any society
or any age, the natural patron is the church. But the theological and
moral confusion from which our society has suffered since the
sixteenth century has much diminished the role of the church as
patron, so that only in this or that corner do poet, philosopher,

131

composer, painter, architect, and sculptor still look confidently to the church for discerning support. In very recent years, true enough, there have emerged heartening signs of a reunion of faith with beauty. Yet in most of the Western world, the scholar and the artist still turn, necessarily and almost unquestioningly, to the secular patron. In our time, secular patrons are of three sorts: the state, the great charitable foundation, and the man of large private means.

Throughout the past four centuries, until fairly recently, the role once filled by the church was assumed by the private patron: the landed aristocrat, the banker, the great merchant or manufacturer. But now that our society feels the pinch of income taxes, inheritance levies, and other devices for economic levelling, this source of benefaction is shrinking. Already it is nearly extinct in Britain—more reduced there, perhaps, than anywhere else in the Western world outside the Communist states. We may be in at the death. Private patronage of the arts and letters of an age always had conspicuous defects, chief among them being the tendency to substitute egoism for spiritual and philosophical and poetic meaning—a fault that may be traced through five centuries, all the way from the great church at Rimini which Alberti built for Sigismundo Malatesta in the fifteenth century to certain American university campuses of the twentieth century.

Yet the taste and generosity of the noble patron, for more than four hundred years, was one of the remarkable achievements of modern civilization. Even in moments of failure and repudiation, the private patron often behaved better than anyone would expect nowadays. When Samuel Johnson wrote his famous rebuke to Lord Chesterfield, that arbiter of urbanity displayed to his friends the overwhelming letter as a model of style and strength, generally conducting himself in the affair more creditably than did Johnson. When Edmund Burke cut himself off from a patron of no especial talents, "Single-Speech" Hamilton, that poor Irish secretary wrote plaintively to Burke as a man forlorn, deprived of his friend and mentor. The great private patrons knew genius when they saw it.

Our generation is dispensing with the private patron. Whether any form of patronage more satisfactory can be developed among us is a question that all friends of culture need to ask with some urgency. For my part, I am disquieted by what observations I have made.

A ruling class, it is said, never loses power except through its own neglect of its duties. Perhaps it is quite as true that a class of patrons loses its prerogatives only when it has lost its taste. As a class, wealthy Americans from the Gilded Age to our era never developed a style or a grand mode; among them were few dilettanti, and fewer virtuosos. Their manner of patronage was passive. Some of them, right up until the Great Depression or even the Second World War, built fine houses: the fashionable suburbs, outer boulevards of our big cities, and quasi-rural counties outside New York are full of these houses still, though for the most part they are a drag on the market, and—as most notably in Grosse Pointe, Michigan, perhaps—every week more of them are demolished to make way for cheaper, comparatively shoddy, and smaller semi-smart dwellings; or else they pass into the hands, successively, of classes lower and lower in the economic scale, until they become little better than subdivided slum tenements.

Still, these houses—Italianate, Georgian, American Colonial, or Old English—were triumphs mainly of the interior decorator and his crew, rather than works of a vigorous architectural school or symbols of a conscious manner of existence. Most of the people who built or bought them remained, in a sense, strangers within these walls. It is melancholy to see many of these houses wrecked, for usually they were handsomely built, of good materials and admirable craftsmanship; some were eminently liveable, but we are replacing them with architectural ephemera that will form the really nasty slums of the future. Yet one feels, having visited a score or so of these big houses, that most of their inhabitants were simply bill-payers, not genuine and discriminating patrons.

Similarly, American people of large means paid a great deal of money for important pictures and sculptures: but they patronized the certified great, dead artist, rather than heartening the painters and sculptors of their own time; and what the chief men among them—Mellon, Frick, Huntington, Kress, and the rest—left to us were museums, not vital and spreading art. So it was, too, when the millionaires turned to the patronage of learning and humane letters: they founded universities, or intellectual museums—and lined their corridors (here I borrow a phrase from Mr. Seymour Betsky) with "museumized intellectuals," doctors of philosophy preserved in amber, with sufficient salaries—quite isolated from the main currents of their time.

Yet what the millionaires did was something; and what is being done nowadays is next to nothing. Tocqueville suggests that while great fortunes encourage great designs in the arts of civilization, a multitude of petty fortunes, decent competences, encourages only mediocrity; for the really rich man has enough money to attempt grand things, while the merely well-to-do man can be nothing more than a prosperous consumer. In part, I think, the failure of the twentieth-century well-to-do man as patron results from the decline of truly great private fortunes. It is improbable that, in the next generation, any Mellon will have the money to erect a National Gallery, or any Duke the capital to found a Gothic university, quadrangles and all. So the failure of the twentieth century is not only one of taste, but also of means.

And we do not seem to be providing any successor to the private patron—no truly satisfactory substitute. We look to the state for patronage, but usually in vain. Here in democratic America, the people grudge even token expenditures upon nonutilitarian culture, such as opera houses or theaters, if the money comes from taxes. Britain, with its Arts Councils, its subsidies to the theater and even the films, has gone as far as any modern free nation in making government the patron. The results, however, have not been heartwarming: Wyndham Lewis, in his vignette of the charlatan teacher of "creative art" in *Rotting Hill,* suggests the pattern.

Here is one real instance of state patronage. During the Festival of Britain, a swarm of cultural experts was dispatched from its London hive to gray old Edinburgh, that the Scots might learn how to show off Scottish culture to the foreigner. Many of these "cultural experts," it turned out, deserved the postwar British epithet of drones, if not of spivs; they knew even less about Scottish art and letters than they did about English. A friend of mine took one of these cultural bureaucrats to Edinburgh Castle, but the civilizational official gazed with lackluster eye from the castle rock across the Old Town to St. Giles' and Holyrood; he knew next to nothing of this bloodstained and famous crag, and cared less. At length, however, his bored glance glided in another direction, and he espied the giant sign of a well-known British multiple store. "Ah, you have a Binns' here! I often go to Binns' in London." Culture was a business by which you got a subsistence; the bargain counters at Binns' were what any rational cultural functionary had an eye for.

Still, Britain retains a considerable body of persons of taste and discernment, and there is active patronage of projects for artistic and historic preservation, if not much intelligent help for new endeavor. Some of the state-commissioned works of art, it should be said, even at state generator stations, are of real merit; and the National Trust for England has no equal anywhere as a conservator of domestic architecture in its setting. The success of such state benefactions and private associations seems to result, nevertheless, from the survival of the heritage of the grand private patron; for the Arts Council and the National Trust are dominated by survivors of the old order of things, aristocratic and professional-aristocratic people brought up in a sense of inherited duty in such matters, and often of trained taste—but now a dwindling breed. When such gentlemen no longer can be found, art and letters may have lean days in Britain.

And the enormous American "private" foundations are not behaving better than is the English state. Utilitarian and humanitarian projects engross the attention of our major foundations: the Guggenheim Foundation and the Bollingen Fund are conspicuous as exceptions. Justification by material works seems to be the credo of the representative foundation functionary. Somehow arts and pure learning embarrass the custodian of industrially accumulated wealth. To contrast the ample resources of the Social Science Research Council with the perennial financial perplexities of the American Council of Learned Societies, I suggest, is sufficient illustration. The first can promise foundations practical results, or at least surveys of possible results; the latter can plead only the intangible merits of truth and beauty. And who'll buy that?

A friend of mine, himself long active in charitable foundations, recently tried to persuade several of our larger foundations to give substantial assistance toward the preservation on a national scale of historical and artistically important buildings. Only one great charitable foundation even toyed with my friend's suggestions; the rest promptly dismissed such proposals as of insufficient "social benefit."

Another friend of mine, also possessed of practical experience in foundation management and familiar with the realm of industry, happened to meet at a dinner a member of a well-known family of foundation patrons; and he set before this patron, tentatively, some projects of a cultural character more closely related to "social benefit" than the plan for historic preservation. Showing some interest, the rich man introduced my friend to the salaried officers of his family's foundation—and also to the head of the family. Soon it became clear to my friend that he was one of the privileged few who had ever penetrated to the inner sanctum of this great family foundation; and to be presented to the foundation's officers by the founder himself ensured a civil hearing.

In the founder's country house, a degree of precedence and protocol almost Byzantine prevailed; foundation officers very like the Grand Logothete and the Supreme Chartulary condescended to sit at table with my friend; and, when presently the founder drifted amiably if vaguely toward the swimming pool, the Grand Logothete and the Supreme Chartulary gave my friend their ears. But their ears only. Within a few minutes, their eyes took on the glazed look of persons who want to get a boring business done with.

This foundation existed to support their dignities. To comply with the law of the land, it was necessary to expend annually a part of the foundation's revenues; and that expenditure, the Grand Logothete and the Supreme Chartulary obviously felt, should be as simple and as safe as possible. Assistance to arts and letters is complicated, even controversial, while making grants for college cafeterias and knocking down old houses to build tall edifices of glass is direct and universally approved. And thinking is always a painful process. The Grand Logothete and the Supreme Chartulary, my friend soon ascertained, preferred to have life be as little painful for themselves as possible.

Now I myself have had some such encounters with the state patron and the foundation patron, and my experience, with a few pleasing exceptions, has been very like that of my British and American friends. The difficulties which Mr. Dwight Macdonald penetratingly describes in his book *The Ford Foundation* seem to prevent even the best-intentioned foundations from filling competently the role of patrons of arts and letters. And I have had also some interesting encounters with certain of the surviving old-fangled private patrons.

A few years ago, for instance, I went down from Rome through the Castelli to Ninfa, which lies in the Pontine marshes, just below the great cliffs of the Volscians. Deserted by its inhabitants seven centuries ago, what with the malaria and the feuds, Ninfa is a medieval Pompeii. The walls of the ancient town, the apse of the cathedral, and bits and pieces of medieval houses still stand. In the old *palazzo publico,* the great princely house of the Caetani has established its country residence; for Ninfa, like Sermonetta on the hill beyond, for many centuries has been the property of the Caetani.

These Caetani princes, who gave two Popes to the medieval church, are the oldest of all grand Roman families; tombs of the Caetani, antedating even the legendary beginnings of their house, were discovered a few years ago beneath St. Peter's. The Caetani are Dukes of Sermonetta; and Marguerite Caetani, Duchess of Sermonetta, is editor and publisher and angel of *Botteghe Oscure,* an experimental literary quarterly in four languages, published in Rome.

No state patron or foundation patron would dream of paying the deficits of a journal like *Botteghe Oscure;* it is controversial, experimental, unconventional. Only an aristocratic or bohemian patron would venture such an undertaking. Besides, literary quarterlies aren't practical; they don't show results. Here in America they exist only by the skin of their teeth, on the most meager of subsidies, in a few of our universities. Yet I think that letters and arts require, in any age, such a stimulus as that given by publications like *Botteghe Oscure.*

A year or so ago I went from Sheffield in Yorkshire out to Chatsworth, the palace of the Dukes of Devonshire, still approached through its splendid miles of park, still perfect in its seventeenth-century grandeur. It is uninhabitable under modern circumstances, and the Cavendishes live at a smaller house nearby. Chatsworth has its pictures and sculptures still, though the Damocles' sword of unpaid death-duties hung over them when I was there. (Since then, by a compromise with the Exchequer, the house with its contents has passed, I understand, to the National Trust.) And Chatsworth has its famous library, though the earlier books have been sold to satisfy previous death-duties.

It is a labyrinth of curious and beautiful things. A lady I know, a member of the family, remembers scooting through the corridors as a child, clutching a great painted ostrich egg she had discovered. That egg had been wondrously painted by Peter Breughel, and her elders retrieved it from her hands with gasps of relief. The Devonshires patronized scholars and artists from the Renaissance down to our time, among them Thomas Hobbes, who acquired from the Cavendish family and its ways his concept of "aristocratic virtue."

At the older house of Hardwick, still standing in these miles of park and farmland, Hobbes commenced his great translation of

Thucydides; and at Hardwick, when he was ninety-one years old, he died. There are scholars working at Chatsworth still; Exchequer or no Exchequer, the Duke of Devonshire keeps the library open to any scholar who needs it. (Hobbes's papers, among others, are there.) But since the last war, four enormous death-duties have been paid upon the Cavendish estates; and perhaps we hear the last chorus of an old song.

Though I have not much more love for the political theories of Thomas Hobbes than I have for those of Karl Marx, the mind of Hobbes, it seems to me, was a much better and more interesting sort of mind than was Marx's. Hobbes did his work at Hardwick; Marx, at the British Museum, where (according to Cunninghame Graham) scholars wear out their eyes and lives for "a pittance a dock-walloper would scorn," and where (according to Gissing) the lavatories bear the legend "for casual ablutions only." The humanism of Hobbes's Thucydides bears the mark of Hardwick; the ideological dogmas of Marx's *Das Kapital* owe something, perhaps, to the reading room of the British Museum. But perhaps I grow fanciful. I mean only to suggest that the "aristocratic virtue" of houses like Hardwick and Chatsworth gave a grace to patronage which great impersonal state institutions and great impersonal charitable endowments do not succeed in emulating.

These desultory observations of mine accomplish no more than to pose a problem. The cultivation of arts and letters is a leisurely activity. For leisurely activity of the higher sort—something better than the taste of the crowd, some measurement more generous than the price of the market place—patrons are essential. We do not seem to be providing a new order of patrons, and we are abolishing with little hesitation the sources of the old patronage. Our immense foundations are intoxicated with humanitarian hustling. Cheerfulness will keep breaking in, nevertheless, and I obdurately indulge the hope that one of these days even the charitable foundations may recognize the principle of culture and the continuing necessity for humane patronage.

And perhaps the church, too, will reassert its old power and generosity in arts and letters. The typical Protestant church building may be a barren ugly thing, with a few distorted concessions to a misunderstood architectural tradition tacked upon its facade; the average Catholic church building in America may be a garish or tawdry endeavor to reproduce faded memories of churches in Sicily or Poland or Ireland, with insipid plaster images, in pastel colors, of saints and martyrs whose final agony is this indignity. Yet vigor is not extinct within the Christian churches, and their intellectual revival, already waxing in strength, may bring also a revival of their sense of dignity and beauty, and with that, a resumption of their part in patronage.

For if every civilization grows out of religious convictions, so every church worthy of the name has the arts and literature as its buttresses, its Dantes and its Giottos. The decline of meaning and hope in letters and arts may have been certain, once the church forsook, or was denied, its old role of patron. And it may have been quite as sure that once the church lost its hold upon the imagination of intelligent men, through its separation from literary and artistic culture, the church's decline as mover of hearts was ordained. For artist and patron flourish in symbiosis.

BEAUTY, COMMUNITY, AND
CULTURE

The Uninteresting
Future

*I*n Avila, the house where George Santayana lived as a child has been knocked down. Though the Spaniards are the most tradition-governed of European peoples, their attachment to the principle of continuity is an abstract devotion: matters of faith and intellect they may defend to the death; but for the great architecture and the historic monuments of their country only a few feel concern.

Santayana's house—described at some length in his *Persons and Places*—was neither very old nor very beautiful; its importance lay in its link with a remarkable man of letters (almost unknown in his native country). But it was an historic house in a pleasant quarter in one of the most interesting towns left to the modern world. To make room for a new housing project, the local authorities swept it away—room for hideous high blocks of flats, jarring with the medieval city and the wonderfully austere countryside, apparently designed by some planner in Madrid or possibly Paris who has not seen Avila. For the windows of these flats near the railway station all face the cold north, from which the winter wind comes across the sierra; and the unfortunate denizens of these hives will shiver out their lives, far less cozy than they would have been in the thick-walled little stone cottages with the low-pitched roofs that have housed most people in Avila for centuries.

In this replacement of beauty, charm, and historic association by modern standardized ugliness, we may perceive one of the great errors of our age. It is not newness, nor even comfort, that can make people content. A professor of art at Brooklyn College, a few years ago, observed that whenever civic planners destroy a neighborhood landmark, they efface one more bond of community and leave men and women rootless and vaguely dissatisfied.

Writing of the English mining villages of his boyhood, D. H. Lawrence says that in those days the miner was not a malcontent—except that he suffered, even though half unconsciously, from the hideousness of the towns he inhabited. The whole temper of a people may be soured by a monotonous and inharmonious environment; what we call "the standard of living" may be very high, and yet the life itself spoiled by nasty buildings, civic schemes not designed on the humane scale, and a general impermanence or shoddiness of homes, public buildings, shops, streets, and even churches.

I recall a passing observation by the Earl of Crawford, chairman of the English National Trust for architectural and rural preservation—and also chairman of the National Gallery, the National Art Collections Fund, and other artistic and architectural bodies: a kind of guardian of English culture. "The future will be so uninteresting," he said, in speaking of the devastation of the countryside, the demolition of great houses and pleasant little cottages, the utter transformation of historic towns, and the whole process of utilitarian "progress" in Britain.

Lord Crawford meant that the men of the future, as things are going nowadays, will be denied the variety of scene, the pleasures of harmonious settings, curious or famous old buildings, survivals of past generations, which have meant so much to civilized existence these many centuries. We seem to be improving away—and priding ourselves upon our ruthlessness—nearly everything man-made that stimulates the imagination or satisfies the eye; indeed, we are rapidly abolishing natural beauties, except so far as they are pruned and tamed in parks.

At a time when, in most of the Western world, we have available ample public and private funds for national and civic improvements on a grand scale, paradoxically we uglify. The bulldozer and the wrecker's ball intoxicate; buildings that formerly would have been spared if only because of their solidity now are obliterated in an afternoon. In the United States, the great private foundations could save much of our architectural and historic inheritance without straining their resources, if they cared; but it is characteristic of our Philistinism that not one of the really big foundations has given any substantial help to the American National Trust for Historic Preservation.

Because of their wretched taste and disregard of ancient buildings, Ruskin told the Victorians, "Posterity will curse you." Yet if the Victorian age had its vandals, at least it often built confidently and solidly; while we of the twentieth century build as if the last trumpet were about to sound. A middle-aged friend of mine, looking at his architect's plans for his new house, inquired whether the roof was well enough designed to endure. "Why," the architect said, in surprise, "it will last as long as you will." A house is becoming a thing as transitory as an automobile.

Every previous era of great prosperity left its mark in an interesting and enduring architecture, private or public—in splendid towns, works of sculpture and painting, and monuments of all sorts. For our part, we build cinder-block drugstores, glass office buildings, and fiberboard ranch-type shanties full of gadgets intended to turn obsolete within two years. Even our sprawling new one-story schools, though expensive enough, are bare and featureless. An age which has no taste of its own ought to conserve what remains of the better taste of other times. Yet we, as if angered by any vestige of antiquity, call a good building archaic if it was erected thirty years ago.

And if we possibly can, we condemn it. At the same time we may be condemning ourselves. More than a decade ago, Charles Baudouin wrote, in *The Myth of Modernity*, of our disastrous infatuation with newness and simplicity: "To simplify up to a certain point is the next thing to hacking down. To restore order, to clean things up, we scrap them, we burn them, and there is an instinct that takes a certain pleasure in so doing. It must be admitted that in the modern liking for a clean sweep there is a trace of this pleasure—should we say of this sadism? It is enough to reflect on the manner in which our cities are treated under the pretext of improving them and making them healthier. In certain hands, this operation is almost as effective as bombardment from the air."[1]

As if the wars of this time of troubles had not already destroyed more than half the important architecture of the world, society proceeds cheerfully to sweep away much of what remains. In Constantinople, Parisian-like boulevards are being hacked, seemingly at random, through the most interesting quarters. "If you like Constantinople now," a Turk said to an English visitor, "you'll like it much better soon. It will be just like your London." He expected felicitations. In Copenhagen, there is a plan for sweeping away perfect seventeenth-century streets to admit motor traffic to what had been, there on the islands, one of the remaining refuges for human beings afoot. In South America, as Gabriel Marcel writes, the devastation of beautiful towns is perhaps worst of all: spared by war, Caracas and Bogotá and many more towns become caricatures of Manhattan or Hollywood. Mussolini did his best to spoil Rome with grandiose highways and gigantic governmental offices; the rich foreigners and Italians who live in the quarter of Parioli show even worse taste. In Fife, the county planners insist on driving a broad highway through the center of the medieval university town of St. Andrews—a highway that leads only to the harborless coast of the North Sea. It is ironical that in the Communist states—particularly Poland—there is some conscious effort to preserve or restore the visible part of their cultural heritage.

As for the United States, we have done more damage to our country's artificial and natural beauty since the Second World War than we were able to accomplish in the hundred years preceding. Our obsession with fast cars and our longing for the prestige of a

[1] Charles Baudouin, *The Myth of Modernity*, trans. Bernard Miall (London, 1950), 12.

suburban house have driven freeways remorselessly through a thousand living communities, destroying everything in their path; these appetites have drained leadership and money out of our cities, at the same time devouring the countryside through subdivisions, so that capitalistic America fulfills the prophecy of Marx that countryside and town must merge in one blur.

"Urban renewal," with federal subsidies, has become a god-term among us. Real urban renewal is desperately needed, and we ought not to begrudge money spent upon it. But the specific projects undertaken often seem better calculated to gratify the contractor and the speculator than to restore urban community. Sometimes decent neighborhoods are abolished to make way for expensive apartment buildings with rents well above anything the previous inhabitants could pay, as in our Bronx development and certain Chicago undertakings. Other sweeping demolitions are ordered by planners who have seen the condemned neighborhood only on a map. The area called Corktown, in Detroit, for instance, was scheduled to be razed as a slum—until the Corktowners, most of them very decent people who own their own homes, shouted indignantly at the city council.

How thoroughly ill-conceived and inhumane much of our "redeveloping" is, has been made fairly clear by the authors of *The Exploding Metropolis;* [2] but few of the planning authorities have mended their ways. Beneath a picture of a typical redevelopment scheme, the *Fortune* critics write: "The city grandiose: Most urban redevelopment projects, give or take a few malls, promise scenes like this: pompous, formalistic patterns that look fine from the top of a tower or in an architect's perspective, but will be an oppressive void to the poor pedestrian. The city is for human beings, not for a race of giant men playing a new kind of chess."

Our grandiloquent "civic centers" rising nowadays in all big cities, generally are spoiled by this same "cult of the colossal," in Wilhelm Röpke's phrase. A generation ago, St. Louis built a windy, arid series of public buildings, rather like mausoleums, as a "civic center." As if this were insufficient, St. Louis now has completed the demolition of the historical river town—which has been in process of being razed for nearly a quarter of a century. In place of an interesting, if dilapidated, old quarter, one sees endless acres of parking lots, the

[2] Editors of *Fortune* (eds.), *The Exploding Metropolis* (New York, 1958).

poor old cathedral standing amid the desolation. Miss Jane Jacobs, in her essay "Downtown is for People" [3] does not spare these misconceived civic centers that actually repel citizens: "San Francisco's, built twenty years ago, should have been a warning, but Detroit and New Orleans are now building centers similarly pretentious and dull, and many other cities are planning to do the same. Without exception, the new civic centers squander space; they spread out the concrete, lay miles of walk—indeed, planners want so much acreage for civic centers now that the thing to do is to move them out of downtown altogether, as New Orleans is doing. In other words, the people supposedly need so much space it must be moved away from the people."

Another instance of recent devastation is the defacement of Long Island, since the war, by bad buildings and superfluous highways. To make room for a spreading population is necessary; but to do it hideously is not ineluctable. The planners now intend to obliterate the eighteenth-century village of East Norwich, in Nassau County, by an immense cloverleaf intersection in the very heart of the place—all to save thirty seconds at the red light. Whither are we hurrying—to more hideousness?

This is the triumph of technology and the death of imagination. Among the several intricate causes of our divorce from continuity and beauty, the ascendancy of utilitarianism and pragmatism in education must be reckoned with. When the mind is constantly fed with the doctrine that only material achievement and "practicality" are worth a man's notice, the just claims of imagination and permanence are denied. And in time men rebel, even though confusedly and irrationally, against the dreary domination of an existence without roots in the past or harmony in the present.

As best we can, we ought to put an end to slums. Yet before we act, we ought to understand what a slum is; and we ought to understand to be sure we are not creating new slums by our very process of wholesale alteration. In the course of a wandering life, I have become something of a connoisseur of slums, visiting many and living in some. Old buildings do not make slums: Oxford undergraduates and Roman princes live in some of the oldest habitable edifices in the world. Poverty, per se, does not make slums: Irish

---

[3] Jane Jacobs, "Downtown is for People," in *The Exploding Metropolis*, 140–68. See also her *The Death and Life of Great American Cities* (New York, 1961).

peasants or Portugese fishermen, with tiny cash incomes, may be among the best and kindest people living.

No, slums are created by a state of mind and a corruption of character. The dilapidation of buildings (and I know certain slums where the buildings are younger than their inhabitants) and the increase of vice and crime and shoddiness follow from the habits of the slum-dwellers. Let me add that once a real slum is established, of course it tends to corrupt the character of many of the people who live there: a miserable environment, depriving men of order and beauty, produces disorder and ugliness in all but the strongest natures.

If you walk the narrow ways of the old Saracen town of Palermo, you encounter great beauty and great ruin. For centuries one of the most splendid cities in Europe, Palermo was badly bombed and shelled in the last war; many hundreds of people live in cellars, stumps of palaces, or picturesque little stone shanties patched together from fallen rubble. And you will find slums: a thousand years of misfortune and misgovernment have made their mark in Sicily.

But also you will find whole quarters that are teeming with decent and cheerful people, clean, neatly dressed, polite. Their living quarters (sometimes a single room for a family) are no larger and no newer than those of the slum denizens; and, like their slum neighbors, they use the public street as their collective parlor. It is not living in a house five hundred years old that degrades a family; indeed, the permanence and beauty of their old house may have a noticeably heartening influence upon them. The real slum is in the heart, and shoddiness there produces shoddiness in the neighborhood. There can be social and material causes of shoddiness in the heart, of course; I am merely trying to suggest that even nowadays we ought not to confound cleanliness with godliness.

It is quite possible for tasteless and unimaginative reformers to produce brand new slums, despite their honest intentions. In the monotonous and drab new country and town housing schemes of Britain, the crime rate has been markedly higher than it was in the shabby old neighborhoods from which the housing-scheme inhabitants often came. If we build towns that are boring—uninteresting because they contain nothing old or curious or varied, and because their style is bad—we must expect the people who live in them, particularly the rising generation, to rebel in one way or another.

At the ancient village of Kennoway, in Scotland, the Fife County Council has resettled thousands of people, mostly miners and their families, in the midst of a lovely countryside. Kennoway itself, founded by those curious Christian eremites the Culdees, away at the misty dawn of Scottish history, was one of the pleasantest places in the country, with venerable little stone houses clustered about a rocky knoll. So the general plan of the Fife County Council was healthy enough; but the execution of it has been miserable.

Those very charms which doubtless induced the council, however vaguely, to select Kennoway as their new housing-scheme site have been swept away by the improvers. The decent little old cottages, most of them, have been condemned as obsolete and demolished or allowed to fall into total decay. Even the street plan has been altered beyond recognition, the new quarters being erected without any reference to the old center. Down toward that great Viking burial mound called Maiden Castle, the authorities have put up a new "town center," modernistic but not modern, shabbily built of concrete that is already cracking after two years of use. A good deal of vandalism troubles Kennoway, and the police sometimes have their work cut out for them; an atmosphere of indifference broods over the new houses, and many faces are sullen. Nearly everyone has a new house, or rooms in the towering blocks of new flats, at a very low rent; but this has brought no content. For the new Kennoway is not a community, but an impersonal and rootless dormitory.

Along the causeway, the old High Street of Kennoway, which twists up and down the little hill where the medieval church once stood, there remain a score of sixteenth- and seventeenth- and eighteenth-century houses. The county council would like to see them all razed, it appears. These form a bond with the past, and the typical doctrinaire planner resents the past. When I was in Kennoway in 1960, navvies were taking the roof off the most interesting and historic of these houses on the causeway—Seaton House, where Archbishop Sharp lodged the night before his murder by the Covenanters. Until three or four years ago, this charming old-fashioned steep-gabled mansion, with its little paneled rooms, was inhabited by a wealthy man. When he moved, the planning authorities suddenly discovered that Seaton House was hopelessly archaic, and they brought it down. One county councillor declared that the process of demolition in Kennoway is all too slow; such old buildings detract from the planned modernity of the new order. But the people who lived along the causeway were reasonably content, I fancy; and the people who live in the new flats are not. Imagination and the sense of beauty are quite as real, and exercise quite as much influence upon the tone and temper of a society, as do refrigerators and improved heating.

In our buildings and our civic plans, I suggest, we are leaving out of consideration some of the deepest human longings. We are becoming the slaves of our own systematic technology. "An ethical and aesthetic culture ought to precede any technical instruction," Charles Baudouin writes. "Technique is only a servant. Pushed to the front, it behaves like a coarse and clumsy parvenu. We have to find its master. But modern humanity is dazzled by technique; it can see nothing else. This is why it is spoiling everything." [4]

Mankind can abide nearly anything except boredom. If we convert town and country into one monotonous realm without interest, historic association, or beauty of design, we may find we have created one great hygienic slum.

---

[4] Baudouin, *The Myth of Modernity*, 141.

Class, Manners, Beauty,
and the Shape of Modern Society

This is my case: there ought to be inequality of condition in the world. For without inequality, there is no class; without class, no manners and no beauty; and then a people sink into public and private ugliness. With Santayana, I believe that beauty is the index to civilization.

Sir John Chester, in Charles Dickens' *Barnaby Rudge,* a gentleman as poor as he is unscrupulous, seems to his creator a loathsome being; and Dickens abhors him as much for his perfection of manners as for his hard heart. Yet in his detestation Dickens does not bear along his readers. When Sir John gives the old innkeeper a very small gratuity but a very large measure of civility, Dickens tries hard to despise his villain for niggardliness. For my part, I confess that in this moment I took Sir John Chester's part: despite his vices, Sir John rose superior to the nexus of cash payment.

It was Dickens who seemed low. The poor gentleman has been the butt of jokes for seven centuries or longer; yet those witticisms have been the children of envy and malice, not the offspring of liberal understandings. Cervantes does not really laugh at Don Quixote's tatterdemalion progress across the dusty plain of Old Castile; for to the true Spaniard, even pure beggary has its peculiar dignity, Spain being full of Edie Ochiltrees even to this day. It is the duke and duchess, rather, and their court who have forgotten the idea of a gentleman along with the dreams of chivalry, who mock the Knight of the Sorrowful Countenance. Like Dickens, the duke and the duchess sink to vulgarity when they confound worldly prosperity with the unbought grace of life.

Now Sir John Chester was what old Thomas Fuller calls a "degenerous gentleman"—that is, a gentleman degenerate from his sires, having lost much of that liberality of sentiment and action which (in Burke's words) "felt a stain like a wound, which inspired courage whilst it mitigated ferocity, which ennobled whatever it touched, and under which vice itself lost half its evil, by losing all its grossness." What Norman Douglas does for Tiberius, I am not disposed to do for Sir John Chester: I am willing to confess Sir John to have been quite as corrupt and murderous as Dickens would have us believe. Yet at the Maypole, when Sir John (or rather, *Mr. Chester*, as he then was) pays John Willet more with a smile and a word than with a coin, he displays the manners that save us from the bowie knife, and thereafter we never can quite convince ourselves that Sir John is treated fairly by Dickens.

Dickens' model for Sir John Chester was Lord Chesterfield; and it is Chesterfield himself who speaks of "the insolent civility of a proud man." Chesterfield rose superior to that insolent civility, even in his patronage of Samuel Johnson and in his reception of Johnson's tremendous rebuke; but it is difficult to hold a brief for Sir John Chester in this particular. For all that, insolent civility is preferable to insolent uncivility, and Dickens himself sketches that part of the unbought grace of life which is bound up with manner when he describes, with an uneasy disapproval, Sir John at home:

How the accomplished gentleman spent the evening in the midst of a daz-
zling and brilliant circle; how he enchanted all those with whom he min-
gled by the grace of his deportment, and the sweetness of his voice; how it
was observed in every corner, that Chester was a man of that happy disposition that nothing ruffled him, that he was one on whom the world's
cares and errors sat lightly as his dress, and in whose smiling face a calm
and tranquil mind was constantly reflected; how honest men, who by instinct knew him better, bowed down before him nevertheless, deferred to
his every word, and courted his favourable notice; how people, who really
had good in them, went with the stream, and fawned and flattered, and
approved, and despised themselves while they did so, and yet had not the
courage to resist; how, in short, he was one of those who are received and
cherished in society (as the phrase is) by scores who individually would
shrink from and be repelled by the object of their lavish regard; are things
of course, which will suggest themselves.

Aye, these things will suggest themselves. For society always will
be disposed toward fawning upon its masters; and it is less disagreeable to pay court to a polished gentleman than to a squalid
oligarch. I have chosen to defend gentle manners upon the least
tenable ground—that is, in the person of Sir John Chester. The
English-speaking world, I trust, will never have to choose between
paying court to someone like the imaginary Sir John Chester and the
real Adolf Hitler or Joseph Stalin; yet precisely that choice,
historically speaking, has already been forced upon a great part of
Christendom. The enterprising talents of Austria and Hungary
fancied that they were oppressed by the emperors and Metternich;
but they came down, at last, to the domination of minds and hearts
quite stripped—unlike Metternich's—of the decent drapery of life,
furnished from the wardrobe of a moral imagination.

Between the decay of manners in our time and the decline of
artistic taste and faculty, there exists some close connection. From
the beginning, the perfection of the arts has been bound up with the
idea of religion and the idea of a gentleman.

Of course the church and the gentleman are the traditional
patrons of the arts; but I mean something still more important: they
are the *inspiration* of the arts. The mysteries and glories of religious
faith have constituted the higher themes of art, since man rose to his
estate; and after religion, the assertions and aspirations of aristocratic society were the principle sources and themes of literature,
architecture, sculpture, painting, music, and the lesser artistic discip-

plines. Now in this past century, religious art in all the world has been so debased that it lies at its nadir—certainly, since the rise of Christianity. One has only to glance at the windows of the typical "religious goods" shop to discern this. The triumph of "naturalism" in letters, the sharp decline of interest in serious poetry, the degradation of architecture by utilitarianism and eclecticism, the ascendancy of "non-objective" and "dehumanized" painting and sculpture, and the cacophony of popular "music" dominated by a banality or a brutality no other age would have endured—these phenomena suggest that the order of persons of taste and feeling which formerly constituted the critical audience of the arts has been deprived of function and nearly extirpated. The "swinish multitude" that Burke feared has routed the traditional guardians of the arts; and this multitude is not composed merely of the poor, but of the vulgar in every walk of life, the proletariat that respects nothing old or high.

This triumph of the mass mind in the realm of art is in part the consequence of certain powerful causes which also crushed or distorted the traditional framework of society; and the revolt of the masses is in part itself the cause of the degradation of beauty. The industrial revolution, for instance, created the modern industrial urban masses; it also overwhelmed those established artistic skills and handicrafts which were joined to traditional art, and substituted new patterns of life and new methods of design for the prescriptive framework of the arts. And the rise of democracy, in part a consequence of the new industrial order, at the same time led to the economic decay of the old classes who traditionally had patronized the arts, and—insofar as democracy, in much of the Western world, took on the aspect of a secular faith opposed to religion—weakened the artistic influence of the church. These causes and consequences are too intricate for adequate description here. Perhaps as good a method as any for apprehending the connection between the decay of traditional establishments and the decay of beauty among us is to glance at the history of architecture in the century and a half since Burke prophesied the disintegrating influence of revolutionary ideas in politics, religion, and the life of the mind.

"We shall have no more Gothic architecture," Anacharsis Cloots wrote to Burke, at the height of the early enthusiasm of the French Revolution. He might well have stricken out the word "Gothic." From whatever causes, true traditional architecture did not long survive the age of revolution. The elegance of eighteenth-century design, which one still can see, square on square, in Burke's Dublin, was succeeded, it is true, by the handsome, if too often **gimcrack,** buildings of the Regency and the Restoration and, in America, the Greek Revival—quite as political establishments had been restored on the Continent or had lingered on, little altered, in Britain and America.

But during the 1830's a radical alteration of architecture for the worse may be observed throughout Western society, paralleling political change. The July Revolution, the Reform Bill of 1832, and the ascendancy of democratic ideas and constitutional alteration in the United States seemed to usher in an epoch of bad taste. Yet the buildings of the earlier Victorian period and of the Second Empire, though ugly enough in many respects, still exhibited a confidence and vigor of execution which is the mark of an energetic society; the Gothic Revival, and the age of "bracketed" houses in America, did not mean the loss of all dignity and substance, despite a manifest affection for the grotesque.

Still another wave of bad taste in architecture, however, rushed across the face of the Western world in the late 1860's, just about the time of the Civil War in America, the Reform Bill of 1867, and the fall of Louis Napoleon. We all know the monstrosities of the age which succeeded, enduring down to the commencement of the First World War—a time in which there was scarcely any decent building, except here and there a respectable neo-Romanesque or neo-Gothic church. A fifth period of architectural decline may be discerned, possibly, about the end of the First World War, enduring until very recent years—the beginnings of collectivistic architecture, the state housing projects of Britain and Europe, and the dreary rows of shabby little bungalows in the United States. Nowadays, we appear to be borne along upon the fierce tide of a sixth movement of architectural alteration, about which I shall say something presently.

Now these stages of architectural alteration closely parallel certain political events; and I am inclined to believe that each wave of alteration resulted in part from the intensification of industrial production and the decline of the old patterns of life in town and country, thus coming as a corollary to the triumph of the masses, rather than as a consequence. But I think also that in part this degradation of taste resulted from the political and economic triumph of the masses, with its necessary eclipse of the old classes which had set the tone of things. One can discern this melancholy relationship most distinctly in Britain, where the reform bills seem like architectural bulls of demarcation. In 1832, the aesthetic influence of the landed gentry was supplanted by the taste of the mill-owners and bankers; their styles, in turn, were thrust aside in 1867 by the lower middle classes and the artisans; and after 1918, the suburbia of the lower middle classes began to vanish before the advance of the new housing schemes of the proletariat. Whatever may be said for or against the ascendancy of the landed proprietors and old families in a nation, in England and Scotland, it is plain as day that their fall from power was the beginning of a progressive degeneration of architectural style and, indeed, of the whole physical pattern of life.

One may see the process being completed by the bulldozers almost anywhere in Britain nowadays. The wreckers' tools today being immensely more efficient than anything available before the last war, British town and country planning officials are proceeding to demolish more rapidly than they can build. One of the more saddening instances is the handsome little old town of Dunkeld, on the edge of the Scottish Highlands. Here, early in the eighteenth century, the ducal house of Atholl built a number of square, white-harled, solid, tall houses with crowstepped gables, all round the square and along the two little streets leading to the cathedral; thus was formed the finest old-fashioned square in Scotland, an architectural composition with no near counterpart anywhere in the world. The rubble walls of these houses were immensely stout and thick, sound enough to last unto the end of all things. But the rent controls, imposed in 1914 and never relaxed, made it impossible for their proprietors to get enough money out of their rent to repair the roofs and interiors properly; and the impoverishment of the dukes of Atholl, through repeated death-duties, led to neglect of these good old houses. They might have been sold to tenants; but the state, or rather the county council, by this time had begun furnishing new houses to tenants at a rent far below the actual cost of building and maintenance.

The houses round the square and the cathedral, then, fell into further disrepair; three or four years ago, they were condemned by the sanitary authorities; and with my own eyes I have seen the bulldozer at work in the square, knocking down one house after the other, on the orders of the county council. They might still have been restored, but the old proprietors had no money for that, and the members of the county council, or their planning officer, refused to do anything of the sort: being pure Benthamites, the county authorities much preferred to let beauty and tradition go hang, and build instead rows of new tenements on fertile farmland at the outskirts of Dunkeld. Scotland lost a beautiful little corner, and a historic one. The sites stand empty and rubble-strewn, like open sores; the whole pattern of life in Dunkeld is altered, and that for the worse, since now the convenient coziness of life in the heart of the town is gone, and people have to travel by bus or private car for their shopping and their participation in the town's life.[1] This is not an extraordinary piece of vandalism and stupidity, but a very common episode in modern Britain.

Since the Reformation, the great architectural boast of Britain has been her splendid country houses, which no other modern nation could equal in number or in beauty; but those appear to be doomed, now, swept away by taxation and the triumph of centralization. In Fife, the county I know best, the process of decay and demolition is checked somewhat by the survival of old ways and by the present lack of motor transportation to the big cities; but it sweeps on dismayingly enough, for all that. Rent restrictions, unearned-income taxes, local rates, and death duties have unroofed a high proportion of the douce stone cottages and houses that stand in the windy streets of Fife burghs; landlords flee from the exchequer as if we were already down to the days of Diocletian. As for the castle and the country house—why, unless some drastic conservative policy arrests the current of affairs, this generation will behold the literal end of them.

I have sat in the ruins of Largo House, where the gracious facade veils the abomination of desolation, the mansion having been unroofed recently after dry rot had eaten it out; I have climbed the broken stair in Pitcorthie House, gutted behind its Ionic columns, for the proprietor has had to surrender it to the housebreaker; I have seen the fireplaces torn out of Melville House and watched the auction at Wormiston. Yet Fife is comparatively fortunate. Out of the four hundred handsomest and most historic country houses in England, ten years ago, two hundred stood derelict; and of those, more than fifty have been pulled down since.

[1] At great expense, the Scottish National Trust now is restoring, as best it can, the damage done in Dunkeld.

More than seventy years ago, W. H. Mallock wrote, in his pleasant book *In an Enchanted Island,* "Now the present, for us in England, what is it? It is a modern order of things, gradually effacing and defacing a traditional: still the traditional order is not yet quite obliterated." Nor is that traditional British order utterly effaced in 1965. Nevertheless, Mallock, before 1889, found it necessary to escape from England that he might recapture beauty and the past. (He chose Cyprus, since devastated by English "improvements," commercialization, and civil war). To Mallock's mind, "the past in England begins before the first Reform Bill, and on the Continent before the French Revolution." Since Mallock's day, the enemies of tradition have hacked most successfully at the chain of continuity, architectural and social and spiritual, in Britain, as elsewhere in this broken world of ours. England is but the symbol and microcosm of our descent toward Avernus.

I suggest here no facile remedies. I am saying, or suggesting, only this: when the faith and the institutions of society which nurtured beauty are fallen into disuse, neither money nor governmental decree can revive beauty. Manners and beauty are not the subjects of fiat. The arbiters of manners and artistic taste, as of morals, Davy Hume said, are men of strong sense and delicate sentiment, whose impressions force themselves upon the wills of their fellow men. Destroy that class of persons, and you destroy manners and beauty.

And, manners and beauty vanished, no culture survives that is worthy of the name. That consummation attained, the best a society may hope for is an endless boredom of utilitarian ugliness; but the odds are that soon such a "civilization" will feel at its throat the prick of the bowie knife.

Cultural Debris:
A Mordant Last Word

We live in a world that is giving at the seams. Sometimes, indeed—especially to a man who travels a good deal—there comes an uneasy feeling that the garment of civilization has already parted and that if one were to tug even the least bit, a sleeve or a trouser leg of our social fabric would come away in his hand. In half the world, the decent draperies of the old order have been burnt altogether, and King Demos struts naked, like the emperor with his imaginary new clothes. When the garment of civilization is worn out, we are confronted by the ugly spectacle of naked power.

160

Yet cheerfulness will keep breaking in. At this hour when Communists and other totalists are busy ripping to shreds the "wardrobe of a moral imagination" (Burke's phrase), certain people of a different cast of mind have turned tailors, doing their best to stitch together once more the fragments of that serviceable old suit we variously call "Christian civilization" or "Western civilization" or "the North Atlantic community" or "the free world." Not by force of arms are civilizations held together, but by the subtle threads of moral and intellectual principle.

Four years ago, I was in Europe participating in two international conferences, intended to help in this pious tailoring. Between sessions, I tramped about England and Scotland with an American friend, an executive in a great industrial corporation. Being something of a classical scholar, my friend collects sixteenth- and seventeenth-century editions of Latin works—particularly Cicero and Seneca—and pokes happily about Roman remains.

We found for his library, in the dusty caverns of Scottish secondhand bookshops, a number of admirable things at trifling prices. There lay the noble elephant folio of Strabo, in two immense volumes, at a mere thirty-five shillings; and the Strawberry Hill edition of Lucan, beautifully bound, at five guineas; and a twelve-volume set of Cicero for a pound. In an age of progressive inflation, one commodity alone remains stable, or actually diminishes in price: good old books. At the devil's booth in Vanity Fair, every cup of dross may find its ounce of gold; but the one thing which Lucifer can't sell nowadays is classical learning. Who wants Latin texts? No twentieth-century Faustus disposes of his immortal soul for mere abstract knowledge. The copies of Strabo and Lucan and Cicero for which a Schoolman might have risked his life ten times over are now a drug on the market. As my friend remarked to me, "These things are cultural debris. It's as if a great ship had sunk, but a few trifles of flotsam had bobbed up from the hulk and were drifting on the surface of the great deep. Who wants this sea drift? Not the sharks. You and I are rowing about in a small boat, collecting bits of debris."

Whether our civilization really retains coherence sufficient for restoration to be possible may be made clear to all thinking men within a few years. If the fabric of our ancient society has declined to the condition of a mere scattering of debris, all the tailors in the world cannot put it aright—nor all the beachcombers live by raking

the sand for its vestiges. The totalists say that the old order is a
corpse, and that man and society must be fashioned afresh, in grim
fashion, upon a grim plan. Yet there survive among us some people
of intellectual power who hold that the wardrobe of our moral
imagination is not yet altogether depleted.

Cant and equivocation dismissed, it seems to me that there are
three great bodies of principle and conviction that tie together what
is called modern civilization. The first of these is the Christian faith:
theological and moral doctrines which inform us, either side of the
Atlantic, of the nature of God and man, the fatherhood of God,
the brotherhood of man, human dignity, the rights and duties of
human persons, the nature of charity, and the meaning of hope and
resignation. The second of these is the corpus of imaginative
literature, humane letters, which is the essence of our high culture:
humanism, which, with Christian faith, teaches us our powers and
our limitations—the work of Plato, Virgil, Cicero, Dante, Shakespeare, and so many others. The third is a complex of social and
political institutions which we may call the reign of law, or ordered
liberty: prescription, precedent, impartial justice, private rights,
private property, the character of genuine community, the claims of
the family and of voluntary association. However much these three
bodies of conviction have been injured by internecine disputes,
nihilism, Benthamism, the cult of Rationalism, Marxism, and other
modern afflictions, they remain the rocks upon which our civilization
is built.

Well, presently my classics-collecting friend and I walked some
miles of Hadrian's Wall, away at the back of beyond in Northumber-
land. Here, for centuries, *Romanitas* and *humanitas* looked north-
ward into barbarism. It is an empty country still, much of it; Pictish
hill forts still scowl almost within bowshot of the Roman masonry.
To the men of the legions, garrisoned here generation upon generation, it must have seemed—even toward the end—that indeed Rome
was immortal; and that the barbarian, however vexatious he might
be in one year or another, never could give the death thrust to a
civilization which extended from Mesopotamia to Pict land, from
Africa to Germany.

Yet in the fullness of time, when the common faith of the Roman
world had lost its virtue, the Picts came over the wall. The end of
Roman civilization was as abrupt as its beginning had been slow.

In material accomplishments, the barbarians never equalled the

Romans; nor had they need to. They possessed the will to endure, and in the end the Romans lacked that will. So all that remains of the material achievement of Roman civilization is some fragments of cultural debris: a few coins, a smashed helmet, scattered beads, a ruined wall, a battered stone head. And as for the Roman moral and intellectual accomplishment, it is sold nowadays for a price not much superior to that of wastepaper.

Once we put some value upon our Roman heritage, and I hope we may do so again. Among us there still are men and women enough who know what makes life worth living—enough of them to keep out the modern barbarian, if they are resolute. If they are enfeebled, and if they cannot make common cause, the garment of our civilization will slide to the rag bin, and the cultural debris of the twentieth century will drift down the rubbish heaps of the future. Not many years of indulgence, I fancy, remain to us. But—as Henry Adams was fond of saying—the fun is in the process.

DATE DUE

DEC 20 '66			
GAYLORD			PRINTED IN U.S.A.